This book is dedicated to all the mums and dads who had the confidence and courage to settle in the newly built River Gardens.

This move gave their children the opportunity to grow up in a rural environment, with the benefit of living in large, modern, and comfortable homes - something that few of those parents had experienced themselves.

Contents

RIVER
GARDENS
by
Lynda Kiss

Published by WordPlay

www.wordplay-publishing.com

Preface

As genealogists we are not gathering cold facts but instead breathing life into all who have gone before. It is not just documenting but writing with pride what our ancestors were able to accomplish. How they contributed to what we are and have today.

Respecting their hardships and losses, their never giving in or giving up, their resoluteness to go on and build a life for their family. It goes to deep pride that the fathers fought, and some died, to make and keep us a nation. It goes to a deep and immense understanding that they were doing it for us. We are the story tellers - we tell the story of our family.

Author unknown

"Census data offers a unique insight into small areas and small demographic groups which sample data would be unable to capture with precision"

The 1931 Census took place in England, Wales and Scotland on the evening of 26/27 April 1931. A question on the usual place of residence was introduced on a census for the first time. Because of the high levels of unemployment in recent years, there were questions about the previous occupations and industries of those out of work for some time, with no prospect of similar employment in the future. Yet, questions on education, dependency, orphanhood, houses being built and places of work were now omitted. As the 1920 Census Act had also provided for the possibility of a census every five years instead of ten, these questions could potentially be re-introduced in a 1936 Census - but this Census never happened.

On the night of 19 December 1942 there was a fire at a store in Hayes, Middlesex. The store, the responsibility of the Office of Works, contained a large amount of furniture, but in addition, it held the Census records for England and Wales for 1931 - that is, all the schedules, enumeration books and plans; they were completely destroyed.

Because of the War, there was no 1941 Census. Instead the 1939 National Register, on 29 September 1939 - which can give only very limited population information - will naturally take its place as a quasi-census for family history researchers. Thus, the 1951 Census, which took place on 8th April 1951, will become more significant for tracking changes in society over the thirty-year period of lost census material between June 1921 and April 1951.

This is a chronicle of family life on a housing estate in the London suburbs from the late 1930s through to the early 1960s. It has been written using documents, photos and memories that I have been able to share with the children and grandchildren of those families who settled on the Estate in the late 1930s. I like to think it will be valuable resource material for Family History researchers of the future.

Lynda Kiss

1935 Map of Poupart's Orchard

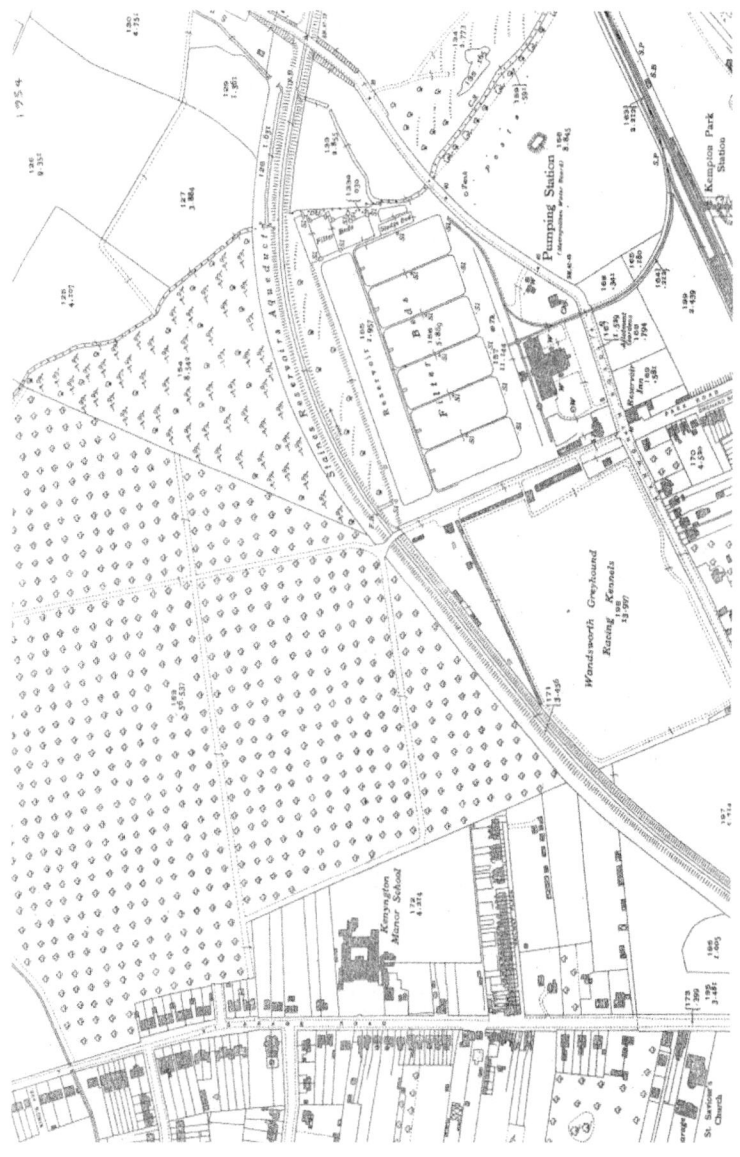

Family Tree

Harry & Clara ROBBINS
10 children

Minnie m. Alfred CHAPMAN
No.51 Ashridge Way

- Brian b.1934
- Derek b.1938

Florrie m. Donald BAIRD
No.101 Ashridge Way

- Keith **BAIRD** b.1943 d.1994
  Married Jill **ROSS** April 1967
- Lilian (Peggy) m. Edwin **RALPH**
  No.49 Ashridge Way
  - John b.1942
  - Christopher b.1953

Mabel m. COOMBES

Albert ROSS m. Rosina JARVIS
No.57 Ashridge Way

Lynda b.1940   Jill Elizabeth b.1947

Wiliam KISS m. Kate Springall
No.1 The Vale

William KISS
m. Christiana Clay
No.185 Ashridge Way

Robert **KISS** b.1939
m. Lynda **ROSS** 26.8.61
No.1 The Vale

- Katie b.1966
- Emma b.1968
- Andrew b.1970

Joan Robbins No.134 AW	Margaret Tresaden 51 B'wood	Evelyn Gregory 127 Ken.Drive.	Florence
Michael b.1942	Zandra b.1951	Trevor b.1943	

PART ONE

Sunbury-on-Thames, Middlesex

In the late 1930s Sunbury-on-Thames[1] was a small village, twenty miles from London; a rural area, its inhabitants were predominantly market gardeners. The Freehold Building & Land Co. Ltd. decided to build in Sunbury, a development of their 'Vincent' houses and called it The River Gardens Estate. The land was purchased from the Poupart Jam Co.[2] and was previously a large orchard of mixed fruit trees. The houses were planned and built during uncertain times; with the Abdication and the prospect of war. Advertisements for the sale of the houses were placed in The Star, The Evening News, The Evening Standard and the Daily Mirror; the national newspapers of the time, appealing to working class families to come and live in the country. They were new three bedroomed houses for sale but for the purpose of investment the Company retained a number of its own properties for rental at 19/6d per week. The properties were designed to a very high standard; containing features usually seen in a house built to a client's specification. They were far in advance of their time and could easily have been exhibited in an Ideal Home Exhibition of the late 1950s.

'Vincent' Houses

There were a total of 230 three bedroomed houses in Ashridge Way and Beechwood Avenue; two double bedrooms and a box room. Woodberry Close had 20 houses and The Vale 16; they were all two bedroomed houses.

The accommodation comprised -

Ground floor:

Kitchens had fitted wooden cupboards with worktops and a larder with a vented window (large enough eventually to house the first little fridges). A gas cooker was provided and a Butler sink. A neat little free standing solid fuel stove in the kitchen, provided hot water and central heating to two of the bedrooms. An iron mangle and a 'Swift's' gas boiler copper were also supplied.

Living rooms were either two separate rooms with fireplaces or one large room with one fireplace and an archway to a wood-panelled dining area. All the living rooms had a serving hatch to the kitchen and a glazed French door to the garden

Doors from the kitchen and living rooms led onto a central hallway, with a flight of stairs to the first floor. There was a cupboard under the stairs containing electric and gas meters. The ground floor had parquet flooring, the concrete kitchen floor was covered with linoleum.

First Floor:

Double bedrooms had fitted wardrobes either side of a recessed space for a double bed. This recess had a lowered ceiling; an architectural feature with an enclosed overhead light with decorative Art Deco translucent glass. Control switches for the overhead light were on the walls on either side. The rear bedroom, had its cupboard situated above the kitchen boiler and contained the hot water tank, making it an airing cupboard fitted with slatted wood shelves.

Bathroom, half-tiled with cream and green tiles and with a

6

green bathroom suite, completed the first floor accommodation. On the upstairs landing was a hatchway leading to roof space with a cold water tank.

The semi-detached houses had a side entrance to the rear of the house and garden, but every house had a door from the kitchen leading into the back garden. A double brick built coal bunker was provided, together with a free-standing iron mangle positioned on the concrete apron at the rear of the house. Gardens inherited at least two fruit trees from the previous orchard - Conference Pear, Victoria Plum, Worcester Apple, some had Greengage and the odd Cherry Tree. Low wooden trellis fences divided each garden, with a 5' fence at the bottom. This taller fence, with matching gate, was strongly constructed with feather edge and arris rail timber and secured the rear access of the properties. Front gardens had similar low trellis fences dividing properties, with a concrete path leading to the front door. A low brick wall either side of small gate completed the frontage of each property. A pavement path encircled the Estate, with a wide strip of grass abutting the road.

The remaining land encircled by the houses, became known by everyone as 'The Orchard'. In due course it provided a wonderful playground for the children who came to live there. Nature soon took over this abandoned part of the original orchards, smothering the old fruit trees with vines and brambles. Wild flowers could be gathered to take home to Mum, tall spires of pink Vetch being the most common. Remnants of the mounds of earth planted with fruit trees, provided large 'bumps' of excitement for fast bicycle rides. Tracks were soon formed crossing from one side of the estate to the other as residents travelled out to the main road - the local shops, the bus stop to Feltham and Shepperton; or commuters walking further on up to Sunbury Cross to catch the train to London or a bus to the towns of Kingston, Richmond and Staines. Sunbury Cross was a junction of six roads; one to the Station and five main roads to these towns. In the centre of the junction was a Clock Tower, a local landmark.

On the Eastern perimeter was land owned by the Metropolitan Water Board and the site of the Kempton Park Pumping Station[3]. The area adjacent to the houses, was thickly wooded, covered in dense vegetation; eventually to become known by the residents of River Gardens as 'The Jungle'. Spiked metal railings protected this private land from public access, and the danger of the fast flowing aqueduct (the Staines Aqueduct) running through the land. The aqueduct carried water from the Queen Mary reservoir at Staines, to the pumping station. 200 million gallons of water a day was fed to this reservoir from an inlet on the River Thames, at nearby Laleham. Steam technology at its finest was housed in the pumping station, the heart of this water treatment works, supplying North London with drinking water. Kempton Park[4] is more familiarly known for its Race Course - the Grandstand overlooked the pumping station's two holding reservoirs and the 12 sand filter beds. A small branch line operated from the Sunbury and Shepperton main line, for the delivery of coal for the pumping station boilers. Only on race days did trains from Waterloo stop at the Kempton Park Station.

Ashridge Way was named after a small, shallow non-navigable local river, The Ash[4]. Beechwood was the name of the building company's office building. On the other side of Beechwood Avenue was a remaining piece of the old orchards and a field. A small stream, a tributary of the Ash, divided these two areas of land and a row of hawthorn trees made a boundary between the field and some gravel pits.

The original rental agreement of Mr and Mrs Kiss, with a weekly payment of £1!

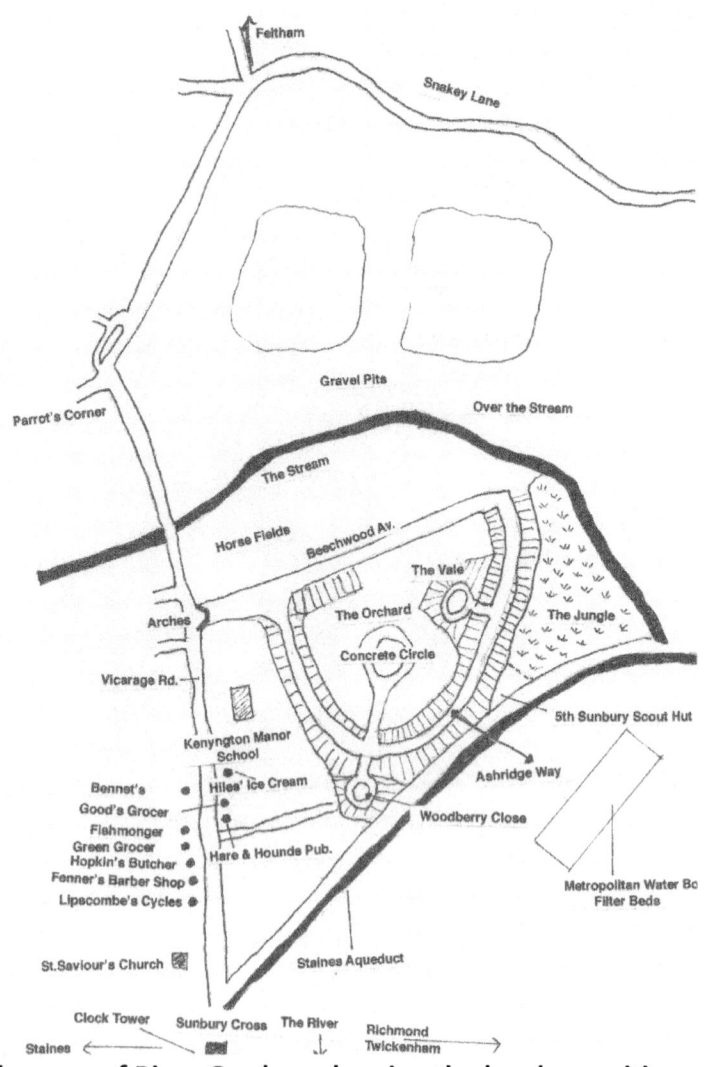

The map of River Gardens showing the local amenities and 'The Jungle'.

FACILITIES

TO THE ESTATE
A quarter of a mile from Sunbury Station the River Gardens Estate may be easily recognised by its distinctive entrance through which is framed an obviously modern development whose neatness is well set off by its background of rural splendour.

SHOPS
It being this company's intention to make the convenient but rural town of Sunbury important and even more desirable to live in from the purchaser's point of view, we have acquired the key position on the main cross roads, where a large and very high-class shopping centre is to be developed, together with a good cinema.

ELECTRICITY
Flat rate electricity is chargeable at the rate of 6d. per single unit. All-in rate allows a standing charge on these houses of 19s. 6d. per quarter, when the charge per unit then becomes ½d.

GAS
Quarterly, 8.7d. per therm ; automatic slot meter, 10.9d. per therm.

RATES
The local Council has assessed the semi-detached houses at £19 and the terrace type at £18. Rates payable at 11s. 4d. in the £ at present are expected very shortly to be reduced to 11s. 0d. in the pound.

SCHOOLS
There are a number of schools of varying types in the vicinity, and a large council school is adjacent to the Estate entrance. Another is expected to be built on the Estate itself.

CHURCHES
Churches of all denominations are within easy reach of the Estate.

TRAVEL
An important factor to all those desiring to keep expenses as low as possible without unnecessary waste of time. Fortunately a good train service throughout the day augmented by a specially rapid service during the business rush hours is given by the Southern Railway from Sunbury Station. This service is, of course, direct to Waterloo. By changing at Wimbledon or Clapham Junction, trains may also be taken to such main stations as London Bridge, Victoria, or St. Paul's.

Fares are reasonable. To Waterloo: Single, 1s. 8d. ; return, 1s. 9d. ; weekly season, 9s. 9d. ; monthly season, £1 14s. 9d. ; quarterly season, £4 14s. 6d.

First train for Waterloo, 5.20 a.m. Last train for Waterloo, 11.2 p.m. Last train from Waterloo to Sunbury, 12.9 a.m.

There is a bus service to Hounslow every twenty minutes; to Kingston every thirty minutes ; and to Richmond every twenty minutes.

Within half a mile of the Estate is Kempton Race Course, while a quarter of a mile beyond is the River Thames, where fishing, swimming, or boating may be enjoyed by everyone.

There is also an open-air swimming pool within easy walking distance of the Estate.

Page 1 of the 'Vincent' Sales Brochure

HOW TO PURCHASE A "VINCENT" HOUSE

Every facility, help, and advice is given to purchasers to choose sites, exterior styles, and interior design and decorations. An expert building staff is at the disposal of clients wishing to incorporate any particular details of their own, when we are only too willing to go thoroughly into extra costs and give technical advice.

Having chosen the site or house, a purchaser then reserves same with a deposit of not lower than £5. The balance of whatever deposit is agreed to becomes payable shortly before possession of the premises is taken. We can arrange mortgages on special terms through one of the leading building societies, so that the purchaser has only weekly outgoings which amount to less than would his weekly rent were he to join the company of our satisfied tenants. Everything is studied and taken into consideration to ensure your satisfaction and the minimum of worry both before and after purchase.

TYPES A, B, C, D, E, and F.

Both in one or two Reception Room Types.   Price from **£495.**

LEASEHOLD.

£25 Deposit. Price **£495.** Inclusive repayments **18/11** weekly.

FREEHOLD.

£45 Deposit. Price **£640.** Inclusive repayments **21/3** weekly.

TYPES A, B, C, D, E, and F.   SEMI-DETACHED.

Both in one or two Reception Room Types.   Price from **£525.**

LEASEHOLD.

£25 Deposit. Price **£525.** Inclusive repayments **19/10** weekly.

FREEHOLD.

£45 Deposit. Price **£665.** Inclusive repayments. **22/2** weekly.

All weekly repayments given are inclusive. In leasehold cases they include ground rent, rates, and repayments and interest.

4

The 'Vincent' House purchase method

A TYPICAL CORNER OF A "VINCENT" DEVELOPMENT

Vincent Houses: complete and on their way.

ANOTHER ONE ELEVATION

The need for linoleum being avoided entirely by the inclusion of solid pine block flooring through the ground floor built upon a 6in. concrete base, and the incorporation of built-in wardrobes reduces the cost of furnishing to a bare minimum, whilst it will be found that with only a living-room fire and the boiler, which will burn coke and all rubbish, the running costs of any " Vincent House " is negligible when compared with other houses of a similar size and larger price.

THE TWO RECEPTION ROOM TYPE

As an alternative type built for those people who find the need for two downstairs rooms as well as the kitchen, this house is built on orthodox design, but with the same luxurious fitments, and in order to provide two rooms of a useful size, extra depth is given by means of a bay window built on to the rear room. This bay has large French windows leading out to the garden.

THE LOUNGE WITH PINE PANELLED DINING RECESS

The brochure showing the lounge and dining 'recess'

MEASUREMENTS

DINING RECESS TYPE

Living Room	..	13ft. 0in. × 10ft. 7½in.
Hall	.. ..	5ft. 6in. × 5ft. 6in.
Bedroom No. 1 ..	11ft. 10in. × 9ft. 10in.
Bedroom No. 3 ..	8ft. 3in. × 6ft. 6in.
Dining Recess	..	7ft. 3in. × 8ft. 0in.
Kitchen ..	..	8ft. 0in. × 8ft. 10in.
Bedroom No. 2 ..	11ft. 0in. × 10ft. 10in.
Bathroom	..	5ft. 6in. × 7ft. 6in.

TWO RECEPTION TYPE

Back Room	..	11ft. 6in. × 9ft. 6in.
Front Room	..	10ft. 9in. × 10ft. 6in.
Kitchen ..	..	8ft. 0in. × 6ft. 6in.
Bedrooms, as above.		

THE MAIN LOUNGE OF THE £495 TYPE

Huge rooms: twice the size that our parents had before!

15

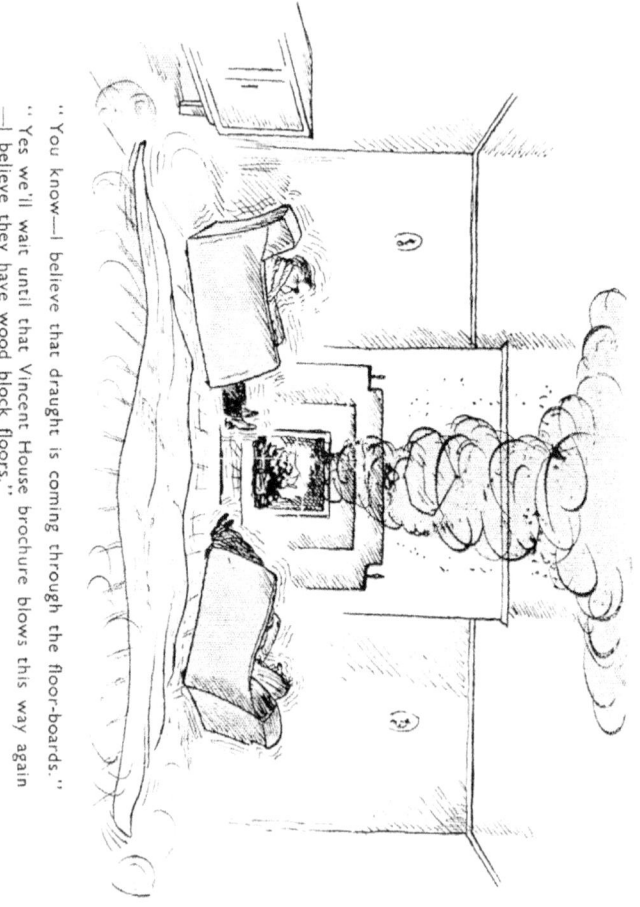

" You know—I believe that draught is coming through the floor-boards."

" Yes we'll wait until that Vincent House brochure blows this way again
—I believe they have wood block floors."

16

" An' I thought that Central 'Eating was something to do with teeth "

17

HOW WEEKLY OUTGOINGS ARE ARRIVED AT

BLOCK TYPE	Price.	Repayments.	Rates.	Ground Rent.	Weekly Outgoings.
LEASEHOLD	£495	12/9	3/11	2/3	18/11
FREEHOLD	£640	17/4	3/11	-	21/3
SEMI-DETACHED					
LEASEHOLD	£525	13/6	4/1	2/3	19/10
FREEHOLD	£665	18/1	4/1	-	22/2

Pinewood block floors; 6in. concrete base; blocks set in layer of pitch; no dry rot; no draughts; no noise.

Central heating for a completely warm house; small fuel bills; no dust; no dirt or smoke.

Built-in wardrobes; no dust collection; brick-built from floor to ceiling; lower furnishing costs.

GARAGE ACCESS. Convenient, costs reduced, useful for collection of refuse, and without which no house in future years will be saleable.

Twelve months' guarantee guarding you against any faults which sometimes appear in any house during its first year, when a certain amount of settlement is bound to take place whatever the price.

Information contained in this brochure does not form part of any contract which may be entered into.

The developer even helped a buyer to budget.

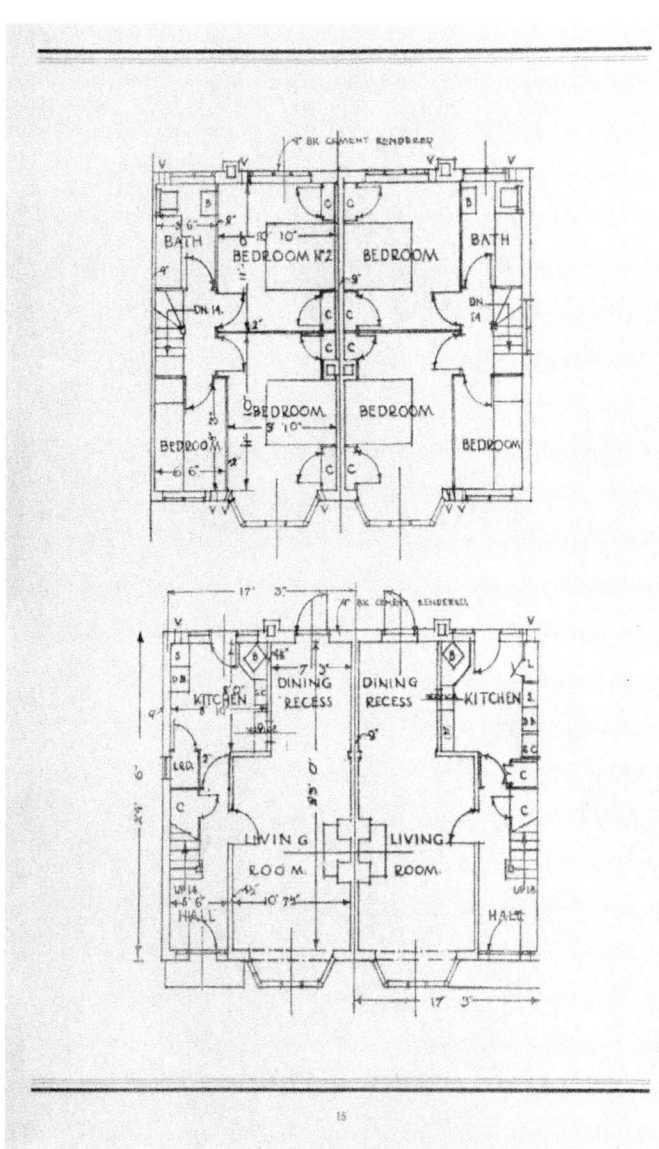

Floor Plans showed just how large the homes were.

19

TO LET

For the purposes of investment this company will retain a number of its own properties for rental.

Houses may therefore be tenanted at an inclusive rental of

19/6 per week

All agreements are for a period of three years and a deposit of £5, returnable at the expiry of the agreement, is payable before occupation is taken.

Three good references are required, and every effort will be made to see that tenants are of a type likely to be desirable neighbours.

Decorations are to tenant's own choice up to a stipulated price for each room.

To those who by necessity must rent we say--You have the best.

And finally: a price to let.

PART TWO

1937-1939 Arrivals

The building of the estate was begun in 1935. By the beginning of 1937 the properties were ready for occupation and the families began to arrive -

Rosina (Rose) Jarvis and Albert Ross were planning to marry in September 1937 in Lambeth Parish Church, London; both were aged 21. Rose was the youngest of a family of 8 children; living with her parents in Lambeth, London, she shared a bedroom with her two older sisters. She worked in Woolworths in the Strand. Albert lived in Covent Garden with his parents and two brothers, they worked with their Father at the Vauxhall depot of W.H.Smith the booksellers. In the early Spring of 1937 with the newspaper advertisement in her handbag; Rose made the 40 minute journey by train from Waterloo to Sunbury railway station. Following the printed directions, she walked down the unmade country road and arrived at the River Gardens Estate. Its entrance was a pair of impressive arches, with roofs of shiny blue tiles, standing over the pavements on either side of Beechwood Avenue. The left-hand arch had the word 'River' in tiled letters and the right-hand arch had 'Gardens'. This road was the beginning of the Estate and led on into Ashridge Way and its two spurs, Woodbury Close and The Vale. Rose reached No. 57 a vacant property that was still available to rent and gazed upon the house where she would spend the next 46 years of her life.

Possibly on same day of Rose's visit, two doors along at

No. 53, Gordon (Paddy) Miles the electrician, was putting the finishing touches to this attractive 'suntrap', one of a pair. As one of the electricians working for the building company, he was commuting from East Cheam every day in his Morris 8. He and his wife Gladys very soon decided it would be much better to live on the job and decided to rent No. 53; an ideal home in which to bring up their new baby boy Basil. Paddy also acted as an agent selling and renting the houses.

The same year as Rose and Albert moved in, Don Baird and his wife Florrie moved into No. 101. They had recently married, making a home together in a flat in Fulham, not far from their parental homes in Hammersmith. Don, although from a working class background, was identified as 'management material' by Square Grip Concrete Ltd. and was relocated out of London to set up a regional office. Don and Florrie decided to buy a new house on the River Gardens Estate. Their only son Keith was born there in 1943. In April 1962 he married Jill Ross from No. 57. Don and Florrie lived at No. 101 for 55 years.

Next door at No. 99 lived David and Clara Keep with their twin daughters. Together with Don Baird, Mr. Keep would cycle to his allotment half-mile away on the Feltham Road. This he did well into old age and even bought a new bicycle when aged 90! He was always self-employed as a jobbing builder; proud of his brickwork on the School balcony, the cosmetic addition that replaced part of the roof damaged by incendiaries during the War.

Albert and Laura Kemp were visiting relatives in the area. One afternoon in 1937 Laura took Emily aged six, the youngest of her five children, for a walk around this new *estate. When they returned home Laura very soon told husband Bert that the £50 pounds they had saved towards a holiday was going to be spent on a property! They lived at No. 90 for many years.*

William (Bill) and Christiana Kiss were married at the beginning of 1938 and their only child Robert was born early the next year. They decided to move from their flat in Chiswick as they wanted a house with a garden for their little son. They arrived at No. 185 - their rental agreement is dated 7th July 1939. Christiana came from Bow in the East End of London, the youngest of a family of 7. When she was three her mother had died in the flu epidemic of 1917. Bill was the only son of William and Katherine Kiss. He had four sisters. He had never had his own bedroom or even his own bed, he slept in a 'Z' chair bed in the kitchen of the small family home in Stratford, East London. One can imagine their joy when they settled into this wonderful house. They continued to rent that house for 44 years until 1983 when they moved to Winchester to be near their son and his family.

On the 26 August 1961 Robert William Kiss married Lynda Ross from No. 57.

Next door at No. 187, the last house on the 'odd' side, Philip (Uncle Phil) Baker and Louisa Baker (Aunty Lou) had bought the property in 1937; the deposit of £25 funded by being a bookmakers runner, quite an illegal occupation. (Especially for someone who later became a local councillor in the 1960s). They had a son John aged 5, his younger brother Chris was born on Christmas Eve 1939 and his siblings Sylvia and Peter arriving in 1941 and 1944. They made the little family newly arrived next door at No.

185 very welcome and became life-long friends. Phil and Lou lived there until old age until their move to sheltered accommodation in Staines.

It appears from electoral records for the period 1937 to early 1939, some tenancies were brief but as the threat of War increased more families moved out from London and the Estate soon filled. Nos. 220 to 240 were the last properties to be built and occupied - a 'Tudor' block of four and a 'Suntrap' block of four. Work was abandoned before the completion of Beechwood Avenue, which would have joined the Estate into a complete circle. The concrete foundations of these planned houses remained in situ until the early 1950s, making a playground surface for children, made aesthetic by the growth of tall spires of vetch and brambles; a sad reminder of the effects of War. It can be seen from these electoral records and those that followed; over 60% of the couples who arrived with young families by 1939 remained living in Ashridge Way, Woodbury Close and The Vale for many years until retirement.

Some still live there today - Margaret Butcher aged 97 lives with her son John who is her carer. Margaret and her husband Stanley ('Mole') came to live at No. 116 in 1938, where they brought up two sons - James born in 1942 and John born in 1944. Their neighbours on one side at No. 114, were Lou and Ernest Gardener, brother and sister - they had not come far, previously living in Shepperton. Ernest spent his life in the Royal Navy and during the War was stationed in Scotland as a Signaller.

Benjamin Dearman and his wife Elsie were the Butcher family's other near neighbour, at No. 118. Ben had poor health suffering from the effects of mustard gas having served in the trenches during the First World War. He worked for Sunbury Council as a road sweeper until his retirement. Many Sunbury residents remember him as a cheerful little man, with his broom and dustbin on wheels, his friendly chat and toothless grin. In 1938 Elizabeth Oestal and her son Donald aged 6 came to live with Ben and his wife. Elizabeth was Ben's sister; her husband had died that year, aged only 38. Eventually Elizabeth managed to obtain the lease of the confectionary kiosk on Sunbury Railway Station on the 'up' platform. She owned this small business for many years, selling cigarettes and sweets to the early morning commuters. Sadly its solitary position on the platform was very vulnerable to break-ins and eventually being unable to obtain insurance, the business was closed in the late 1960s.

Extended families also arrived - Grandparents - not sure who arrived first in some cases but we do know that William and Katherine (Katie) Kiss followed their son Bill out of London and took up residence at No. 1 The Vale before the War.. They were able to share the two bedroomed house with their daughter Joan Robbins. Her husband Cyril had been called up in the Army but in 1942 when their son Michael was born, Joan obtained the tenancy of No. 134. Margaret another daughter was married from her brother Bill's house (No. 185) in 1939 and with her husband Michael Tresaden found a little flat above the Food Office in Green Street Sunbury. Michael was also called up into the Army but was captured at Dunkirk, where he suffered severe injuries to his legs but was safely repatriated in 1946. Together with their little girl Zandra, they eventually came to live at No. 51 Beechwood Avenue, when the road was completed in the early 1950s as part of a Council house estate. Evelyn

Gregory, the youngest daughter came with husband Greg and son Trevor to live at No. 127 Kenyngton Drive, another part of this estate. The Kiss family had now relocated to Sunbury from London's East End!

The Beavan Boys arrived at No. 125 before the War. William and Bertha brought their family of three boys - Gordon, Peter and Paul to live next door to their Grandparents George and Margaret Beavan and Aunt Annie Beaven at No. 127. Three more little boys arrived in later years, John, Tony and Terry. William Beavan grew up in Somerset; continuing his country bred husbandry skills, he kept goats on a fenced in area on the 'Orchard', as well as keeping a small heifer tethered somewhere in the 'Jungle'. The baby goats were happy to be picked up and nursed by children playing in the 'Orchard'. Inevitably, being goats, the adult animals often either chewed their tethers or pulled the stake out of the ground, making their way to the nearest easily accessible garden where they ate everything in sight - flower, vegetables, shrubs etc. Ben Richards living next door at No. 123, heard on many occasions someone knock on the Beavan's front door early in the morning and ask "please come and get your goat out of my garden!" The boys used to milk the nanny goats in the evening in an enormous shed at the bottom of their garden and Ben together with his friends, would lean over the fence, poking their heads through the window, and receive a squirt of warm milk aimed at their faces. Goats milk is special, particularly rich and nutritious; a TB patient living at No. 57 became very grateful to the Nanny Goats at No. 125. The Beavan family emigrated to Australia in the 50s. Auntie Annie Beavan cared for her elderly Father when Mother died and she continued to live at No. 127 until she died when in her 80s.

Bill Norman can remember when his family arrived at No. 88 the houses were still being built further down on the even side. As a little boy of 6 he asked one of the workmen if he could have a paint brush and some paint to paint one of the front doors!

The Inseal family moved into one of these remaining houses - No. 206 with their son Frederick. Henrietta and Frederick Inseal were married in the Spring of 1935 at Caxton Hall Registry Office - the famous venue for celebrity weddings in the 1950s/ 60s. Their daughter Eileen was born at No. 206 in 1939. Albert and Eleanor Britten moved into No. 97. Very soon after their son Arthur and his wife Winifred settled into No. 162 and their daughter Marie and her husband Dennis Wiley decided to come to live in Ashridge Way as well at No. 218, bringing their daughter Moya with them. Her little brother Donald was born in 1940 and their cousin Roger Britten was born the same year at No. 162.

The Bread Winners

A large proportion of the families who settled, were young married couples. Several arrivals in 1937 were newlyweds but by 1938/39 many arrived with children; more often than not, just one child. Family history shows several of these parents had grown up in large families; probably an overcrowded environment with limited income. Many relocated from the London area because they wanted the opportunity to live in these wonderful modern homes, paying a rent they could afford. Their aspirations were for their children to have advantages they had never had. To rear their families in the country away from the smoke and bustle of a metropolis and be a small family unit - many who arrived with one child never did increase the size of their family. With the threat of War and the uncertainty of what sort of life they would be bringing children into, at this time many couples had made the decision to have just one child. Bill Kiss was thrilled with the arrival of his third grandchild in 1970, a grandson to carry on the name - his daughter-in-law remembers him saying -

"We do not care how many children you have - we did not want Robert to be an only child but you did not know what sort of World you would be bringing children into".

How did these husbands and fathers provide for their families, what did they do to earn a living? Women rarely went to work once they married. In the Civil Service it was a condition of employment that a woman was unable to continue work upon marriage. Muriel Gridley a midwife and nurse came to live at No. 117 in 1938 with her husband Leslie, but she did not resume her career until after the War, when the children John and Jennifer were older. Minnie Chapman also did not work while her boys were small but when they started Junior school she got a job with F.A. Good the local grocer. She worked there for many years with Mrs. Cramp from No. 25. Mrs. Higgs was a teacher at the Nursery School in Beechwood Avenue and Dorothy Crabb at No. 108 was the school secretary. This was not until her two boys John and David were old enough to attend the school. Her husband George was a lorry driver.

Peggy Appleby was a qualified cook and she too started work when Brian her son started school; she was in charge of the school kitchens. Thomas Appleby had brought his family from the NE of England to live at No. 212 and walked every day to work at the British Thermostat Co.

Peggy asked her neighbour Mrs. Inseal to help her as a cook at the school but as her little girl Eileen was only four years old she did not feel she could take the job, but the headmaster allowed Eileen to start school early. A group of older girls were assigned to look after her during dinner and tea breaks and she was thoroughly spoilt.

It appears the majority of the men continued their previous occupations; their places of work being in the London Metropolitan area and not a great distance to travel. They were a mix of blue-collar workers - skilled or unskilled manufacturing and white-collar workers - jobs situated in an office environment.

The British Thermostat Co.[1], was an expanding company and in 1931, moved to new premises at Sunbury with a payroll of 60. In 1934 they collaborated with Rolls-Royce[2] to produce an experimental thermostat for their cars and a prototype thermostat system that became the forerunner of nearly every system fitted to the Merlin[3] engines during the War. Other equipment was produced for the Spitfire[4] and Hurricane.[5] A new railway station, Upper Halliford Halt was opened on May 1st 1944 between Sunbury and Shepperton stations, to serve this aircraft components factory. It had concrete platforms with brick shelters. During the War the Company grew considerably with a payroll of 2,300 and many of these workers lived on the Estate and the jobs were considered reserved occupations. Sidney Neal lived at No. 30, he was an early employee; later his wife Doris also worked for the Company and they cycled together to the Factory every day. Stanley Butcher at No. 116 was a foreman with the Company.

Half a mile away at Spelthorne, the Anglo Iranian Oil

Company[6] had a small laboratory development at Spelthorne. George Muir had re-located from Scotland to work there. He lived at No. 95 - Ben Richards remembers him as a "crazy Scotsman, with a thick Scottish accent, impossible to understand". Always late for work running across the 'Orchard'. Edward Morris from No. 173 also worked there. These laboratories expanded considerably in the late 1940s and had a large canteen for its employees; after the War several mothers found ideal employment as waitresses, just three hours work, 11a.m.- 1p.m. fitted in perfectly with child care. Christiana (Chris) Kiss and her friend Lilian Norman worked there for several years serving lunches and waiting at tables; they made sure their neighbours had good helpings! When the company became British Petroleum working conditions changed and Chris found a job with the American company RCA[7] newly arrived in Windmill Road; an area fast becoming the industrial centre of Sunbury. She soon learned how to solder printed circuit boards for the Company's record players. Women's fingers were ideally suited for this delicate manufacturing process, making equipment for the burgeoning record industry.

Cantrell & Cochrane[8] a soft drinks company, was a local employer; Harold Dee was a Director of the company and lived with his wife Doris at No. 181. The drinks processing building was next door to another company, 'Sundeala',[9] a factory making insulating building board; sheets of solid, hydraulic-pressed, interwoven wood-fibre. The emissions from its manufacturing process created a dusty, pungent atmosphere in that area of Sunbury near the Clock Tower. Ben Dearman was employed by the company but was one of the 500 employees made redundant after the devastating fire that swept through the factory in the mid-

30

1950s.

Bill Kiss had completed his apprenticeship as a sheet metal worker with the Ford Motor Company[10] at Dagenham. When he took his wife and newly born son to live in Sunbury he was working at Chiswick for H.J. Mulliner[11] coachbuilders making Rolls Royce car bodies. When War was declared this type of metalwork ceased and he was assigned to aircraft manufacture with Vickers Armstrong[12] at Weybridge; a reserve occupation. He returned to work at Mulliner's after the war. A memorable job was making the running boards for the Rolls Royce car given to Princess Elizabeth as a wedding present, by the Royal Air Force. His close neighbour at No. 179 Laurie Opperman also worked on aircraft but with a repair company on the Staines Road.

Edward Thompson lived at No. 34 with his wife Dorothy and worked for London Transport. Edward worked in the offices, as did Leonard Marsden at No. 121 but Leslie Hopkins at No. 131 worked for London Transport but for the Underground Railway, in their workshops at Acton. His was not a reserve occupation and he was called up to serve in the Army. His wife Nellie and son Graham, born in 1940, remained living at No. 131 during the War. At the bottom of their garden Les had built a garage - it had unique double doors - two recognisable London Transport Underground train doors, however, they did not automatically slide open! Next door to the Hopkins at No. 129 were the Clayton family; William worked at Kingston Power Station,[13] the coal-fired generating station on the Thames. His wife Violet kept the flowers fresh at the local church, St. Saviors.

William Kiss (Grandad Kiss) was a nightwatchman at the

greyhound kennels in the Hanworth Rd. *In later years his grandson Robert, setting off on his early morning paper round, can remember seeing Grandad returning home from a night's work, wobbling along on his bycycle with a great sack of straw taken from the kennels, bits dropping off all the way home to No. 1 The Vale. He kept rabbits.*

Dorothy Linter's Dad was a gas fitter, also a reserve occupation but sadly Eric Linter died in 1946 of a brain tumour leaving his wife Winifred and little daughter Dorothy to live alone at No. 202; although Winifred's sister, Mary Wilkins and her husband Edward lived nearby at No. 111.

Jocelyn (Josh) Owen and his wife Cicely lived at No. 69. Josh worked for Wilkinson Sword the famous razor blade company as a sales representative - "never paid for a shave" as he was one of the Company's testers for their razor blades and had to make weekly reports on their performance. John Beard was a bricklayer and often worked away from home leaving his wife Hilda at No. 164 with their daughters Marjorie and Janet. He had served his apprenticeship working on Battersea A Power Station and was employed again in the 1950s on the building of Battersea B Power Station. The two individual power stations were built in two stages but in the form of a single building. Battersea Power Station[14] is the largest brick building in Europe.

Sunbury was only a 40 minute railway journey from the heart of London and a few residents commuted daily.

Albert Ross caught the fast 'workmen's train', travelling Monday to Friday to Vauxhall where he worked as a clerk in the distribution offices of W.H.Smith the booksellers. These trains were often overcrowded and ran at inconvenient times but the fares were very cheap. Albert encouraged a work colleague, Bert Oxspring to bring his wife Lily to live on the new estate. They were a newly married couple living on a house boat on the River Thames at Mortlake. They moved into No. 2 The Vale and lived there for the rest of their lives. They never lost their love for life on the River and kept a small motor launch moored at Sunbury. Rose and Albert shared weekend river trips, together with other neighbours. A redundant naval barge was acquired, installed in the garden of No. 2 and Bert spent many happy hours converting it to a pleasure craft, but it never reached the river! They had no children but doted on their spaniel dogs.

Bert and Albert were both members of the Printers Union[17] and a couple of times a year had the opportunity of a Saturday night's work in Fleet Street, travelling up to London in Bert's little car. On those nights they could earn the equivalent of a month's wages, cash in hand, tying up parcels of Sunday newspapers and loading them into the early morning delivery vans. Several of Albert's near neighbours also worked in the print trade and commuted to London. Across the road at No. 68 lived Arthur Knights, his wife Evelyn and their son Ron. Arthur worked for the Daily Mirror newspaper in Fleet Street . Albert Norman at No. 88 worked for Iliffe & Son; the company owned by the newspaper magnate Sir Edward Iliffe. Starting in his teens, he worked 49 years for the Company until retirement.

Jack Ambrose at No. 110 worked in the City and could be seen every morning walking to the station smartly dressed in a pin-striped suit. Jack lived with Eddie Chapman who was artistic, and worked as a window dresser in the West End. They were a gay couple. Frederick Inseal was a Telephone Technician working in London but he rode his bike there and back to save the fare. He later got a transfer to Walton-on-Thames Telephone Exchange working on the Test desk; much nearer to home. Julie Andrews lived in that area and one of the stories Fred related was when her Mother rang complaining about her telephone not working. Fred told her that quite a few lines were down due to the weather and she would have to wait her turn.

She was quite indignant – "but Julie Andrews is my daughter and we need the telephone. I demand you fix it now!"

Fred replied -

"I don't care who the bloody hell lives there, you can bloody well wait your turn'.

William Morgan was definitely something in the 'City'. He wore a dark suit, a bowler hat and had a finely rolled umbrella and strode with a military bearing very fast. It was like the Royal Army Green Jacket Regiment ceremonial march - 140 paces a minute his feet did not seem to touch the ground. He lived with his wife Gladys at No. 240 the last house, his was a long march up Beechwood Avenue to the main road on his journey to the station. They had no children. In 1941 John Richards and his wife Winifred had originally signed the lease for Mr. Morgan's house, but changed their mind and managed to secure No. 123 nearer the middle of the Estate. They had one son, John (Ben) born in 1940. Mr. Richards cycled to Weybridge with Bill Kiss to make aeroplanes, but after the War he opened one of Sunbury's first restaurants 'The Galleon', previously there had only been cafes.

The film studios at Walton-on-Thames was originally started by the early film pioneer, Cecil Hepworth, but in 1926 the studios were bought by Archibald Nettlefold, and renamed the Nettlefold Studios[15], making comedy silents until it was upgraded to sound in the early 1930s. The decline of the British film industry meant that only a few films were made in the late 1940s on a modest budget and to keep the studios afloat, an 'open door' hiring policy was deployed. Bill Kiss earned extra money by working at the studios as a film extra, as did several other neighbours, it was just a cycle ride away and good fun. Bill appeared in 'The First Gentleman' - a photograph in costume, has pride of place in the family album. Had there been no 'open door' hiring policy it would not have been a problem for Bill, as he held a British Actors' Equity union card. He was no stranger to having more than just a day job. He had met his wife Chris on the dance floor, in his part-time occupation as a solo vocalist with some of London 's West End big dance bands. 'Billy Kiss' was a crooner - Equity required its members to have unique professional names! He received bookings by postcard, from Jack Anderson, the Band Leader with a note of the songs to rehearse for the Friday or Saturday night performance at various functions in London hotels. He was once second billing with Gracie Fields. Equity was the last of the closed shop unions in the UK and made illegal in 1988.

Wilfred Simmons was the Postman and lived at No. 232 with his wife Ivy and only child Sheila. One or two families were self-employed - John Bernadout and his wife Kathleen were hairdressers, and some owned shops. Edward

Edwards with his wife Belinda lived for a short while at No. 156 and ran the local hardware shop; we would think of it today as a D.I.Y. shop - known always as 'Edwards'. The Giles family at No. 19, Stanley Giles, and the Gunner family No. 20 Beechwood Avenue, James Gunner; together owned a small stationery shop called 'Stanley James'. They sold post cards, envelopes and writing materials and printing orders were taken; it was conveniently situated next to the Post Office on Sunbury Parade. Harry Kinzett lived at No. 115 and had an electrical shop, selling TVs. He tinkered with anything electrical and his back garden shed was crammed with radios, early TVs, clocks, and irons. In 1954 he sold the Kiss family a 10" table model Marconi in time for the FA Cup Final - Bolton Wanderers v Blackpool. Bolton were leading Blackpool 3-1. Every time the crowd roared, when Stanley Matthews went on the attack for Blackpool and made all the goals, the Kiss family did not see anything, they had sound on vision!

PART THREE

Outbreak of War – More Arrivals

Sunday 3rd September 1939 at 11.15 a.m. on BBC Radio the Prime Minister Neville Chamberlain announced "England is at War with Germany".

Ted Ralph and his Mother Mabel, at their home in Paddington, listened together to the radio broadcast and sirens blew within minutes. Everyone was out looking skywards for aeroplanes, expecting bombing to commence at once, but of course nothing happened until the next year.

At No. 101 Ashridge Way Don and Florrie Baird were privileged to have a telephone, because of Don's managerial role at Square Grip. When the War was announced on the radio that fateful morning, Florrie's sister Minnie Chapman and her husband Alf, by pre-arrangement telephoned the Bairds. They confirmed they would drive out to Sunbury to stay with them. The Chapman family occupied an upstairs flat in a three-storey house near Ravenscourt Park in Hammersmith. Remaining in London was too great a risk for a young family. The Chapman's half cooked Sunday joint was hurriedly removed from the oven, and packed into their little Austin 7 car, along with a few other essential items. That afternoon Alf Chapman drove his wife Minnie and their two little boys, Brian aged 5 and Derek 18 months, to join their relatives in safety in Sunbury.

They stayed with Don and Florrie for several weeks. They very soon made enquiries to see if there was a vacant house in the same road. No. 51 became available, they signed the tenancy agreement and very soon moved in with their boys.

Minnie and Alf Chapman lived there contentedly for the remainder of their lives.

Alf was a boot and shoe repairer with a tiny shop in Hammersmith. After the move to Sunbury, every day except Sundays, he cycled the 11 miles there and back in all weathers; suffering each winter with bronchitis. During the War, on a journey to work, he was hit by shrapnel from an exploding bomb. He went to help others who were injured in the blast; then someone pointed out the back of his shirt was soaked with blood. He had not realised he himself was injured; he had a huge gash in his shoulder and spent several days in hospital. His little Austin 7 car was garaged throughout the War as fuel was hard to come by, there were just the odd special outings. He had married Minnie in 1933 and worked for her father who was also a boot repairer. When his father-in-law became an invalid, Alf took over management of the shop and the car was purchased to take his in-laws out and about. In later years his boys passed their driving tests in their Dad's Austin 7; Derek failed his first test because the hand break seized on.

Ted and Peggy Ralph were both still teenagers when they married in 1941. They began married life sharing accommodation with friends at 'Little Venice' an area of Paddington, London; however Peggy's aunts Minnie Chapman and Florrie Baird visited in the Spring of 1942 and urged them to join them in Sunbury where bombing was not considered to be a danger. They made the move with their newly born son Jon and stayed with Florrie and

38

Don for two and a half years. During this period Ted Ralph was called up into the RAF but invalided out in 1944 having been diagnosed with TB. Aunt Minnie learned from her neighbour Mrs Hutton that she was giving up the tenancy of No. 49 so Peggy and son Jon moved in. A few houses along, at No. 53, when the building on the Estate halted, Paddy Miles' electrical skills were needed in the aircraft industry. During the War he was wiring Spitfires at the Feltham Aerodrome, less than a mile away, as the crow flies.

Eva and Wilfred Fletcher arrived at No. 120 Ashridge Way in 1940. They had left London to escape the bombing and wanted to take their little daughter Doreen aged four away from danger. Wilf, a policeman was assigned to the police station at Hampton but being an ex-Grenadier Guard he was soon called up. Charles Robinson had moved his family into newly built No. 220 soon after the birth of his daughter Jose in 1938. He owned a factory locally that made airplane wings. Susan his second child was born in 1942 but Charles abandoned his little family in 1944

Edward (Ted) Higgs was in the Mounted Branch of the Metropolitan Police and when War was declared the decision was made to move all the horses to safety to Kempton Park racecourse and to the Royal Mews at Hampton Court. Ted and most of his colleagues assumed the War would only last six months, after which they would be moved back to London. Because they thought their stay was short term, Edward and his wife Florence did not buy No. 177 for £490 but took out a tenancy to rent at £1 per week and settled into their new home with their young son Brian. They both hated being away from London but as time passed they accepted their new life in Sunbury as did other members of the Mounted Branch who moved to houses locally or to Hampton.

Ernest Clark was a local boy brought up in French Street, Sunbury. He moved to No. 32 when he married Olive, who came from Shoreham-by-Sea. He served in the RAF during the War as an aircraft engineer and was stationed in Canada. After the War he worked locally at London Airport for BOAC as an aircraft engineer and their daughter Jacqueline was born at No. 32 in 1947.

At No. 206 Fred Inseal was very soon called up by the Army. He had joined in 1929 when he was 16 years old, having told the authorities he was 18. He was posted to India, the Northwest Frontier in the Mountain Artillery and served there for six years. Fred junior recalls "he often said they were the best years of his life. He was called up at the outset of the War with other colleagues who were in India with him. He was a paratrooper in the Royal Signals so he carried the portable radio with him when he jumped out of the plane. He was taken prisoner of war.

Requisition of Houses

In 1938, in anticipation of the coming war, the Directorate of Lands and Accommodation of the Ministry of Works, set up a central register of accommodation. This was used during and after the Second World War in the acquisition of land and buildings for the service departments and in the allocation of accommodation for civil servants. In the National Archives, the records Requisition, Compensation and Settlement are registers relating to property taken over by the State during the Second World War in seven counties, including I.O.W. However, similar registers relating to the other counties, including Middlesex, do not survive. Such a pity, as these registers give addresses, dates of requisition, derequisition and claims for compensation - amount of claim and sum agreed. From the electoral rolls of 1939 and 1945 it appears that several houses on the Estate had shared lettings, occupants having as many as four different surnames. Sunbury companies were engaged in War work - British Thermostat Company's increased workforce would have needed accommodation. Many families shared their home taking in lodgers, some for many years -

"Uncle Charlie lived for many years with the Neal family at No. 30".

No. 57 was a house that was requisitioned during WW2. In the Spring of 1940 Albert received his call up papers for the Army but was allowed to delay reporting for duty until June, after the birth of his first child Lynda Ann earlier that month. He enlisted into the Royal Signals Regiment, and in July 1941 was posted overseas, as part of the 8th Army. He was away for four years. Rose took her new baby to Lymington in Hampshire, to stay for the period of the War with her parents and other members of her family. The house was requisitioned and all the furniture and personal belongings were stored and locked in the main bedroom.

Reality of War

Sunbury very soon knew the reality of War - a bomb fell on the Running Horse public house on the 29th November 1940. The pub was situated at Sunbury Cross; several people were killed and considerable damage done to the up side of the railway station. The railway station did not get rebuilt until 1969. On the same night there were a lot of incendiary bombs in the region of Ashridge Way.

There were hundreds of prisoner of war camps spread across the Country during the War and one was at Kempton Park Racecourse. It was a large complex encompassing all the pre-existing buildings with 212 tents within the prisoner compound. These men were sometimes seen under guard around Sunbury working on house building in other parts of Sunbury. It was claimed that in the attics of some of these houses swastikas had been painted on the walls. An escape attempt by a couple of prisoners resulted in one being drowned in the gravel pits. Towards the end of the War the children used to frighten each other as they played in the 'Orchard' - "don't go down that alley, Hitler's down there, he has broken out of the concentration camp"

In July 1943 there was another drowning in the gravel pits. On the 14th September that year Bill Kiss was awarded a certificate by The Royal Humane Society "for having on the 11th July 1943, at personal risk, gone to the rescue of a child who was unfortunately drowned in a Gravel Pit at Feltham Hill Road, Sunbury, Middlesex, and whose life he gallantly assisted in attempting to save".

1944 was known as the mini blitz and the residents of Ashridge Way had first hand experience of this time; two near misses with HE (high explosive) bombs. One fell in the field next to William Morgan's house No. 240, and the other on the other side of the 'Stream' which separated two fields. Neither caused much damage -

"in fact they merely formed ponds in which we went fishing for tadpoles".

Hitler ordered Goering to retaliate against our bombing so

for three months the Luftwaffe carried out quite a lot of raids with a small degree of success.

No house in Ashridge Way was directly hit during the War, unlike Heathcroft Avenue. This was another housing development by the same builder. Same type of houses but the road was nearer to the Clock Tower and just around the corner from the Sunbury Cross shopping parade. Soon after War was declared, the Father and Mother of Albert; Minnie and William Ross, moved to Heathcroft from Drury Lane in London. Also his older brother William Ross, wife Elsie and baby son Peter. Minnie and William had a lucky escape; the three houses adjacent to them were demolished as a result of a direct hit by a bomb on one house and neighbours were killed.

On the 22nd February 1944 the local school, Kenyngton Manor was hit by a number of incendiary bombs. Fred Inseal was six years old and remembers going to school that morning seeing the fire and smoke in the distance thinking it was the Sundeala factory. "When we got closer it was our school! I think we said 'good old Hitler!'. Anyway we went into the playground expecting to see the school burnt down. There were unexploded incendiary bombs laying around which some of us tried to pick up. The firemen got us out of the playground pretty smartly. I think we had a longer summer holiday that year."

Brian Higgs can vividly remember standing in the road with his Dad looking in the direction of the school but thought it was the local pub The Hare & Hounds next to the school that was on fire.

"Because of the partial destruction, we could only attend

school for three or four ½ days each week. The roof to the school hall was completely destroyed. It did not prevent the holding of the normal morning assembly, albeit within a roofless hall."

Jose Robinson was in the air raid shelter at the end of Beechwood Avenue, opposite the Baker's house No. 187, when the school was hit in the air raid.

"I remember seeing the flames from the door of the air raid shelter. Thought I would not have to go to school but they patched it up and we went as usual".

At Easter, a couple of months later Robert Kiss started school age 5. Both of these children remember having to go into the brick built air raid shelter. Jose recalls -

"It had chairs with horse hair seats that scratched the back of your legs and bunk beds. All the Mums made a beeline for them so they did not have to have their children on their laps. I also remember it had a paraffin heater which stank."

When no longer in use after the War, Derek Chapman remembers they were a good place for playing cowboys and indians.

V2 Attack

At 0410 hours on September 15th 1944, a single stage ballistic V-2 rocket, 46 feet long, weighing 13 tons, with a one ton Amatol warhead, struck the Sunbury Water Board's filter beds at Kempton Park with an impact speed of about 1800 mph. It was 215 yards between the impact point and the nearest houses in Ashridge Way. Quite a close call considering how far it had travelled; it is known that the rocket was launched from Wassenaar on the coast of Zuid Holland. This was just seven days after the very first V-2 attack on London, causing casualties at Chiswick.

Brian Higgs was seven years old at the time, and remembers as a family they had been visiting the Grandparents overnight, with the consequence that their house No. 177 was empty of people.

"Having been called back by the Police as a result of the incident, my first and really very vivid memory was the sight of the absolute mess in the road as we walked from Beechwood, round the corner to our house and into full sight of much of Ashridge Way.

The road was covered in broken roof tiles, glass and much other debris. Most of the glass in the windows to the front of the odd numbers and rear of the even, was missing.

Some had been replaced with insulating building board - how fortunate that this was manufactured locally. Other windows were still being hacked out and cleared. It was very much a hive of activity"

"In the small bedroom on the front of the house, my little brother David had his cot and this was completely covered in glass. We had a piano in the sitting room. This finished up with glass splinters all over the polished surface and furthermore, the blast took the sound board away from the cast iron frame and split it from top to bottom. It was really quite a mess all round and never the same again!"

Ben Richards remembers that night; it was very hot and his Mum had them sleeping in the back bedroom with the windows wide open and not as usual downstairs in the dining alcove under the Anderson shelter, where they would have been buried under shards of glass.

The Poultry Club

For the period of the War, there was a large corrugated metal hut on the grass circle opposite Woodbury Close. It was a store containing chicken feed and meal, grit, straw and seeds. The authorities supplied these items to encourage the keeping of chickens and rabbits and to grow food. The River Gardens Poultry Club was formed by the residents to administer the distribution of these supplies. A committee was formed and regular meetings took place. Phil Baker became known as 'just a minute Baker'; he was on the Committee and he repeated this phrase quite often trying to keep order at lively meetings.

It was very common for everyone to have a few chickens but when it came to eating them not many could wring their necks. For Bill Kiss this was not a problem and he provided this service for many of his neighbours. He was an authority on the keeping of chickens. His Rhode Island Reds won prizes at local Fur and Feather shows. When son Robert was older, he accompanied his Dad on fishing trips to the gravel pits. After two or three hours they would return with scores of small perch; boil them up in the garden, mash with bran meal and feed to the chickens. Wilf Fletcher at No. 120 kept ducks on his pond in the garden and Don Baird and David Keep were not the only ones to have allotments throughout the War. Many of the men spent their spare time together "down at the allotment" growing food to supplement rations.

A considerable number of the men living on the Estate

were in reserve occupations and therefore served either in the ARP (Air Raid Precautions) or the Home Guard during the War. An experience that created a bond, as did the war experience in general. Women also served, Sybil Deeks was Chief Air Raid Warden. Sybil lived with husband Sidney at No. 65 which was just round the corner to the ARP Hut, sited next to the seed store. The ARP Wardens kept their supplies of gas masks, pre-fabricated air-raid shelters, and sandbags. Paddy Miles a neighbour of the Deeks was also an ARP. They were issued with a set of overalls, Wellington boots and a black steel helmet and expected to be on duty three nights a week; responsible for the upkeep of the local public air raid shelters and the maintenance of the blackout. They patrolled the roads calling out if necessary

"Put that light out"

"Cover that window"

Operational from 1940 to 1944 the Home Guard was the defence organisation of the British Army during the War. Local volunteers otherwise ineligible for military service. Bill Kiss was Quartermaster Sergeant in the local Home Guard. His superior was Major Moore, who was the Chief Sanitary Inspector at Sunbury Urban District Council (still in post in 1954 when Robert Kiss, joined the staff in the Treasurer's Dept).

Ted Ralph although away in the RAF from mid-1942, was hospitalized after contracting malaria and tuberculosis while in North Africa and invalided out in 1944. By then it was becoming clear the war was being won by sheer effort and determination and he noticed an almost tangible increase in community spirit everywhere when he returned after those two years away. The pre-war community he had known in Paddington did not compare with the strength of feeling during and for a while after the war in Ashridge Way.

River Gardens survived the War and its young families had become a community closer and stronger as a result of living together through the crisis and their mutual support through austerity.

PART FOUR

1945 – Returning to Normal

The end of the War – WW2 Allies formally accepted the unconditional surrender of the armed forces of Nazi Germany - the act of military surrender was signed on 7th May in Reims, France and on the 8th May in Berlin.

Ted Ralph remembers the night of the 7th May when Victory was declared. To celebrate he recalls putting out a candle in a jam jar in the porch of No. 49. Many people along the street were doing the same thing and the idea spread. Some had coloured their jam jars red, white and blue. All the candles were from the emergency supplies held in case of bombings, now they were no longer needed! This candle light routine continued for several nights.

On May 8th in London, crowds massed in Trafalgar Square and up The Mall to Buckingham Palace where King George VI and Queen Elizabeth, accompanied by the Prime Minister Winston Churchill, appeared on the balcony of Buckingham Palace, before the cheering crowds. Among the crowds were Rose Ross, her sisters and their children, having travelled up from Lymington in Hampshire, to join in the celebrations. Lynda Ross age 5 remembers being there, sitting on the shoulders of her Uncle Bill King, looking up at the Palace, and being part of the cheering crowd. Later that day Rose caught the train to Sunbury. Holding tightly to her Mother's hand, Lynda has another memory of standing on the doorstep of No. 57 hearing her Mother say to the gentleman who answered the knock on the door.

"I need my house back - I shall want to move back in next week".

Jose Robinson remembers the celebrations at the end of the War. There was dancing in The Vale, on the grass circle in the middle. A makeshift platform was made for the piano that did not have to be carried far from it's owners home; Will and Katie Kiss at No. 1. Living just along the road at No. 220, Jose heard the music and although only 6 years old, went to the event on her own. Her Father had recently abandoned his family and her Mother was too upset to take her but Jose remembers getting up on the platform and singing "Don't sit under the apple tree with anyone else but me!" The street party, organised for all the children, held at the same venue as the cricket match; is remembered by some of the older boys, Brian Higgs, Basil Miles and the Chapman boys. Towards the end of the event all the children piled into back of Mr. Crab's open lorry for a drive around the streets. Great fun, however they only got as far as Job's Dairy when the lorry broke down and everyone had to walk back!

As part of VE-Day celebrations, some residents on the Estate decided to have a celebratory cricket match over the 'Orchard'. Ted Ralph remembers playing in the match, together with Don Baird, Alf Chapman, Paddy Miles, and others. Albert Shailer from No. 136 captained the team. They had to improvise for a wicket as the only suitable pitch was the little bit of straight concrete road leading to the 'Circle' but it sufficed and it was a memorable event.

The return to normality for those who kept the 'home fires burning' must have been a wonderful feeling of relief but for those who had been away at war or in captivity, normality took longer to achieve. "going home was hard, not just for the person returning but often for those who opened the door". What was the impact on small children when a gaunt stranger came through the door after years away, announcing that he was 'Father' and evicted them from Mother's bed? At No. 57 Rose and Lynda awaited Albert's return. He embarked from Calais on the 29th June and on the 30th began a month's leave. His army record does not show where his fighting ended but his medals earned during the four years he had been away, were for action in Egypt, Palestine, Syria and Italy. It must have been the first morning he was home; Lynda's first memory of her father was seeing him in bed with her mother and he produced a present for her from under the bed - a banana! It took a long time for her to accept this strange man and for her to call him 'Daddy'. For a time there were many upsets when she refused to do anything he told her to do.

Much later that summer Fred Inseal arrived back home to No. 206. This returning Prisoner of War was greeted by crowds of neighbours celebrating his safe return.

Terry Pattinson who lived at No. 28 Beechwood Avenue will always remember -

"When Mr. Inseal came home we all had flags and bunting out all along Beechwood and gave him a great cheer when he came marching back"

Fred's children, Fred junior aged 9, and little Eileen who was 6, remember the day their Daddy arrived home. Who was this strange thin man, all arms and legs, sitting in their kitchen, his right hand covered in bandages; it looked as if it hurt the way he was resting it on his lap. Both of them

51

crying, they were frightened, not used to seeing a man in their house. The chimmney sweep was the only man they remember being allowed indoors!

Sergeant Major Inseal as a paratrooper, had been taken prisoner at the Battle of Arnham in May 1944, imprisoned in STALAG prison in Fallingbostal Germany. He never talked about the experience and when the children asked how he injured his hand he said "I put it up to see which way the wind was blowing". For the rest of his life this badly injured hand was an impediment and little fragments of shrapnel continued to surface through the skin right up until he died. In 1956 the Inseal family emigrated to Australia. When they arrived in Brisbane Eileen remembers her Father's first job. The only one he could get, was in a railway yard carrying heavy fishplates. "He wrapped a cloth around the little bit that was left of his damaged hand as it became covered in blisters carrying the heavy metal fish plates". As an experienced telephone technician he eventually got a job in the Brisbane Telephone Workshops fixing phones where he remained until retirement. He loved playing golf and Eileen made him a special protective mitten for his injured hand with wide pieces of elastic sewn in a loop which he would fit over his hand to hold the golf club in place.

At No. 183 Thomas Commerford did not come marching back; he left a widow Phyllis, son Vincent 14 and two daughters Veronica 12 and Margaret aged 9. He was killed on the 19th August 1944 in the Western Europe Campaign following the Normandy landings. He fought with the Royal Armoured Corps in the 8th Kings Royal Hussars.

Phyllis remarried but remained living at No. 183 for many

years. Their son Vincent became a Catholic priest.

Gladys Robinson struggled on alone to make ends meet, caring for her two little girls at No. 220. It was in 1938 that her husband Charlie Robinson had brought the family to live in the newly built house. At that time he owned a factory making airplane wings. Gladys cleaned the little nursery school at the top of Beechwood Avenue, and lit the school's boiler every day; two of her three jobs; she worked at the wireless factory during the day. Because she had jobs at the Nursery, Susan aged 2, her youngest daughter, was allowed to attend the nursery. Jose her older sister would take her on her way to school. Life was very different for children then, parents would not now send a six year old and a two year old off to school on their own. Mrs. Higgs was a teacher at the nursery school.

After school Jose would collect Susan from the nursery school and they would go to the house of their neighbours the Finch family at No. 224. Doris and Herbert Finch had twin daughters Coral and Deborah. The girls were all of a similar age and after school would play cards together until Mrs. Robinson came home from work. Sometimes the Parker family at No. 226, would take the children in but they had a large dog, a Chow, which used to chase the Robinson's dog 'Buddy', a collie. Once 'Buddy' was chased right into his own house, through the front door and up the stairs where a fight ensued on the upstairs landing. Eventually Gladys saved enough money to buy the house from the builder and in 1947 she took her little girls and moved away to make a fresh start.

William and Gladys Paynter lived at No. 228. In 1940 their son Joseph married Lilian Parker, the girl next door and they set up home at No. 22 Beechwood Avenue. Joseph's sister Gladys had married William Kitson in 1939 and they lived at No. 61. Both of these young couples did not have families until after the War. As close neighbours, Gladys and Rose Ross became life-long friends, as did their daughters Susan Kitson and Jill Ross who were both born in 1947. A small post War baby-boom arrived in Ashridge Way but there remained a considerable number of children who grew up as an only child.

Most of the men remained in the same places of employment, some returned to their previous occupations. For example Bill Kiss moved from working on aircraft to return to his skills as a panel beater within the car industry. Some went even further afield - Edward Mintern from No. 210 went to work on the Ground Nut scheme in Kenya. He sent for his wife Ivy, and sons Derek and Keith and the family emigrated permanently in the early 1950s. Son Derek was conscripted into the Army to fight the Mau Mau but did return to live in England in 1990.

The River Gardens Poultry Club was disbanded after the War ended and replaced with River Gardens Sports & Social Club. One of the first social activities they organised was a day trip to the coast - Littlehampton. Brian Higgs can remember there were seven coaches, or charabancs as they were called then, all lined up near the remaining brick arch at the top of Beechwood Avenue. Just after the War, one arch had been demolished by a confrontation with a Fears coal lorry.

"It was pouring with rain when we left, but having got to the other side of the South Downs, it changed to sunshine. A great day, most of us had not seen the sea before.

Unfortunately one vehicle broke down whilst we were at Littlehampton, so the occupants just spread themselves amongst the remaining six coaches in order to get home."

A highlight of each summer was the Estate's sports day held on the spare ground the other side of Beechwood Avenue, opposite No. 187 where the Baker family lived. Slow bicycle, egg and spoon, obstacle, and sack races; long and high jump, with sprints and distance races. Great involvement by the adults; setting the course and adjudicating results, tremendous fun on the part of the children. Cash prizes were given for the first three places but in 1948 a silver cup, was awarded to the child who accumulated the most points. Brian Thompson from No. 143 was the first recipient; the Baker children won it for the next three years. Sports day was disbanded when the Council began to build houses on the spare ground in the early 1950s.

Billy Kiss – Big Band Vocalist

Minnie Chapman and Florrie Baird

Sunbury Juniors Football Team 1948/ 49
(Ashridge Way)

Back Row: Brian Thompson (143) Brian & Mike Marshall (169)
Middle Row: Fred Inseal (206) Colin Oldacre (147) Ginger Collins (224)
Front Row: Brian Appleby (212) Derek Mintern (210) Robert Kiss (185)
Missing: Alan Dobson (159) Alan Thompson (143)

Kenyngton Manor School

Sunbury Swimming Pool

1950 Council House Terrace – Beechwood Avenue

5th Sunbury Scouts – 50th Anniversary

Basil Miles, Graham Hopkins, Titch James, 'Skip', Bob Kiss, Eddie Edwards, Derek Chapman, 'Gaffer'

Tricycling for Britain!

Always at attention, and always looking smart.

**Ted & Peggy Ralph with son Jon and their dog Curly
at 49 Ashridge**

1946 Kenyngton Manor Infant Class

Cavendish Rd. VE Day Street Party

Wedding at No. 57

1957 Jon Ralph and friend with little brother Chris Ralph

1953 Inseal Family

Back Garden at No. 192
Freddie Saville on left, Jeannie Clark with her brothers

PART FIVE

Voices of the Children

Childhood memories of Robert Kiss, Lynda Ross and their friends - 1946-1956.

"We played in the street a lot and had long skipping ropes with seven or eight children all skipping together" Jose Robinson

The streets were for playing in - hop scotch chalked on the large paving stones outside your own house or games of tin can copper, hiding in the front gardens or down the alley ways. In winter fantastic ice slides were made on the sloping camber of the road between the lamp-posts. Hardly ever had to stop for passing cars, only delivery men, and then not at the weekend or at the end of the school day. Job's dairy electric vehicles were early morning visitors, the coal lorry, perhaps the vegetable van on Thursdays or the delivery van of F.A. Good the local grocery store. This was the shop where most families used their ration books. Mums would take in a written order for the week and it would be delivered to the house. If you had gone on an errand to the shop you could watch the sugar being weighed into blue paper bags, the top neatly folded down and the same for biscuits. Or the butter patted into a measured ration; for a family of four it was a ¼ of a pound. It was half a wrapped bar of New Zealand butter, the cut end protected with a square of greaseproof paper. The baker had a hand cart; Derek Chapman got a job with him once, he seems to remember his pay was in doughnuts.

Few residents owned a car and if they did they were

garaged in the back gardens and not parked in the road. The Thompson's at No. 143 always had a car, brand new Vauxhalls. On summer Sundays, early in the morning around 6.00 a.m. the Thompson family all piled in the car, slamming the doors and set off for a day at the sea. John Maudesley living opposite at No. 176 got so fed up with these disturbed Sunday mornings, he ran up and down his concrete path with his lawn mower to give the Thompson's a taste of their own medicine one morning when they did not go out. Harold Dee was a Director at Cantrell & Cochrane so he had a beautiful maroon Riley. Harry Kinsett drove around in a Humber Super Snipe, a big car for a small man, who wore a wide brimmed trilby hat - a James Cagney look-alike. Doug Costa had a Ford 8, Paddie Miles and Ted Higgs each had a Morris 8. Freddie Boden at No. 196 had a Austin Coupe with a rear boot upholstered seat for two. On one occasion the family invited Robert Kiss aged 9, to join them on a day trip to Bracklesham Bay but his Dad would not let him go - he considered it unsafe sitting in that boot. It wasn't until 1953 that Bill Kiss bought his first car with money from a season's winnings on Shermans Fixed Odds football pools. Robert his son remembers the arrival of one of the registered envelopes from Shermans containing crisp white £5 notes. The car was a 1936 Ford 10 saloon, bought for £100 from Arthur Hourd at No. 2, in 1953.

A different mode of transport, which we did not mind interrupting our play, was Bob Hiles' ice cream cart. Pulled by his pony, it would work its slow passage around the estate. He would ring his hand bell announcing his arrival. It was wonderful homemade creamy ice cream scooped from churns on the swaying little wooden cart. It had not come far from where it was made; his premises were next *to the school in Vicarage Road and he only delivered in one or two nearby roads. He kept his horses in the fields opposite Beechwood Avenue; these fields, the remaining pieces of old orchard, were part of our other childhood adventure playground. The gravel pits were out of bounds but of course there were adventures there too and the stream was a powerful magnet for any child.*

The Stream

1948-1956 John Butcher No. 116

When the stream and I first became acquainted in 1948 she was simply teaming with life: newts, frogs, frogspawn, tadpoles, smooth newts, great crested newts, sticklebacks, grass snakes, water beetles, water boatman, pond skaters, snails, dragonflies, mayflies and aquatic plants of every kind. The water was clear. The bottom was muddy. We would make fishing nets from a length of bamboo pole, a piece of wire and our mother's old stockings and see what we could catch. We would tie a rope to any convenient tree branch and swing to and fro across the stream. We would run and jump and with luck reach the other side of the stream without getting a boot full. One day the 'Gang of Four' - Jeff Shailer, David Crabb, my brother Jim and me - were playing over the stream when we suddenly became rather hungry. I was sent home to get some sandwiches. On the way back, while crossing a muddy, makeshift dam, a grass snake slithered off the dam and began to swim down stream. As quick as a flash I grabbed it's tail and lifted him into the air. A little boy can attract quite a following while proudly walking down the street holding a two-foot long grass snake at arms length. Strangely my mother was not as pleased as I thought she would be. She told me to "take that thing back to where you found it, immediately".

That stream was probably happily bubbling from its source to The River Thames for a hundred thousand years.

The Gravel Pits

The gravel pits were fraught with danger and out of bounds to the children but of course they went there. Very, very deep with sheer sides from the excavation of gravel, if one fell in there was no escape. A workman's barge, a flat bottom craft with 3' high sides, was tied up near the extraction crane. One day in summer, probably a bank holiday, either the Whitsun or August holiday, with no workmen around; a dozen boys, aged between 8 and 14 clambered aboard this boat and tried to propel the craft across the gravel pit. Brian Appleby was standing on the prow and suddenly fell in. Bob Kiss saw him go right under and one of the older boys Peter Elkington from No. 190 had the presence of mind to grab the oar and poke it at Brian when he surfaced and Brian grabbed it with both hands. Several more pairs of hands helped pull him aboard, so lucky, as he could not swim. Eileen Inseal remembers her brother Fred was one of the boys who used to get on the barge and a few times it would break away from its moorings and how worried she would be about how they would get back, but they always did.

The Jungle

The Jungle was out of bounds but Jacqueline Clark from No. 32 remembers playing with girl friends in the unfenced area on the outskirts, sometimes venturing through the railings to the land owned by the Water Board.

"The game was to get to the stream without the 'Water

Board Man' seeing us. If he did we would all run like mad to get back through the railings to safety."

The boys were more adventurous and made regular sorties into the Jungle. Fred Inseal had a shotgun and with his gang would often "go hunting animals". They would take turns to use the gun but one day a younger boy, Freddie Saville from No. 194 got in the way and was peppered with shot. His facial injuries resulted in him losing the sight in one eye. Fred Inseal's sister Eileen remembers, when Freddie Saville came out of hospital, her mother prepared a party for him; cooking lots of cakes and making jelly and blancmange, so the boys could let him know how terrible they felt and how remorseful they were. However, he refused to come to the party so Mrs. Inseal sent a tray of everything she had prepared to his house. He obviously was unable to forgive the boys and from then on avoided them like the plague. Another tragedy occurred in the spring of 1946, when three year old Alan Hopkins from No. 131, probably following his older brother Graham and other children at play, wandered into the Jungle and was drowned in the culvert taking water to the filter beds at the pumping station. The community were stunned and parents lectured the children on the dangers of this water course, even if you could swim there was little chance of getting out from the deep sided concrete culvert full of fast flowing water.

The Orchard

The orchard, the area of waste land enclosed by the houses, was a safe playground and had the benefit of being not far from home and Mother's call. Fast bike races could be taken on the paths that crossed from one side to the other. They had undulating surfaces where fruit trees *had previously been planted; it was exciting riding 'the bumps'. Flowers were always available to pick for Mum, Pussy Willows and Catkins and tall spires of pink Rosebay Willowherb; the first plants to brighten London's bomb sites. The goats owned by the Beavan family were tethered at the back of their house and there were often baby kids who loved to be cuddled and played with. Secret camps could be made in the bushes, out of sight but within earshot of calls from Mother when it was time to go home. The boys would be away on the field playing football using jackets or jumpers for goal posts, playing until dark, in the end the ball could not be seen in the dusk and eventually they had to go home. Cricket was best played on the concrete circle. On windy days this clear space was also the best place for flying kites. If a child appeared with one then everyone had to have one too. Old ones were retrieved from cupboards or Dad's were pressed into finding sticks, brown paper and sticky tape to get one made as quickly as possible. Great fun was had sending messages up the string, seeing who had the biggest kite and which flew the furthest distance. John and Chris Baker's kites from No. 187, were memorable. On one occasion, a perfect kite flying day, the wind direction was towards Vicarage Road, away from the Jungle and the houses. The Baker's kite was very big, with a long tail of paper bows. Once airborne it was so well balanced that it floated high in the sky, maintaining the same height, but travelling further and further away each time extra lengths of string were added, almost disappearing from view. At lunchtime they tied it to their fence, had lunch and returned to find the kite still in the same position in the sky. Eventually the weakest link in the string gave way and the kite disappeared from view.*

November 5th, Guy Fawkes Day - each year many days

would be spent building a huge bonfire on the land behind No. 187. Another bonfire was always built by the children living at the other end of the estate, opposite Woodberry Close. Always a competition to see who could build the biggest. A guy was made and put on the top. All the families would gather around, sharing fireworks. The boys would throw fire crackers and jumping jacks to frighten the girls and catherine wheels would be pinned to the wooden fences. Later the children gathered together roasting potatoes and chestnuts in the embers. Chris Baker at No. 187 had a tortoise as did several of the children. They started a tortoise club and met regularly at Chris Baker's house. Each contributed a penny towards buying olive oil to shine their shells. Eileen's tortoise was Horace and her sister Marion's was Jemima. Life was never lonely there were so many children of all ages to play with.

Minnie Chapman from No. 51 was the person who continued to organise the annual Littlehampton coach trips for many years, right up until the early 1960s. By which time many families had become car owners.. Minnie also ran a Christmas Club during the 1950s. Neighbours would save each week a sum they could afford. It was recorded in their own notebook and signed by Minnie. Her sister Florrie Baird ran a National Savings club for the local children and the Christmas Club money was safely kept at the Post Office with the purchase of National Savings stamps. Two weeks before Christmas the money was paid out. One year Rose Ross, having collected her Christmas savings from Minnie, when she counted it at home, realised it was £1 short. Embarrassed at having to question Minnie about the difference, she quickly returned to No. 51 to have the money checked again. In order to iron out the £1 notes as they were very creased, Minnie had put them through the mangle. On investigation there was the missing £1 note stuck around the damp rubber rollers of her mangle.

Coronation Day

2nd June 1953

Mrs Deeks at No. 65 was viewed as the elder stateswoman in that part of the Estate, by the younger mothers who were her neighbours. Early in 1953 when the Nation's plans were being made for the Coronation, these mothers approached Mrs. Deeks to ask her to organise a street party for the children on Coronation Day. She agreed to head an organising committee and money had to be raised to pay for the food, paper hats and a small commemorative gift for the children. Rose Ross was on the committee and much against her will, her daughter Lynda was sent every Saturday morning to knock on doors and collect 6d for each child, from the families who wanted their child to go to the street party. On the day, those who could watched the ceremony on a television, neighbours sharing their sitting rooms. Lots of the school children from the Estate had the opportunity to go to the Festival of Britain in 1951 but for the Coronation only one child from each school year was chosen to go to London on that special day. Stands on the procession route were allocated especially for these school children. Although it rained for most of Coronation Day, our street party was held later in the afternoon and the sun came out.

Education

Fred Inseal started school at Kenyngton Manor in 1940 -

"I still remember my teacher when I was in the infants. Her name was Miss Torpey.

I remember when she taught me and two or three other children to say 'there are thirty thousand feathers on a thrushes throat'

That was because coming from Lambeth we had a bit of a cockney accent. Eventually when we pronounced it properly she gave us each a bag of sweets."

Kenyngton Manor School

Headmaster - Percy Dutton September 1940 - April 1956

The headmaster in charge during one of the most important and difficult periods in the school's history. The war years, when many of the male staff were called up and the work of the school was often disrupted by bombing raids and other wartime emergencies, were immediately followed by the transition from a senior to a secondary school, required by the 1944 Education Act and the first post-war raising of the school leaving age in 1948. These stresses and changes took place under conditions of economic stringency more onerous than present day educational restrictions.

"Those of us returning from the services in the years 1945-1947 were immediately impressed by the way in which Mr. Dutton had maintained educational standards and school spirit throughout the war years, despite serious fire damage to the building in 1944, constant timetable interruptions and the employment of many temporary staff."

"Under his guidance we began the task of creating a secondary school, expanding the curriculum and building up inter-school and community links. Many pupils went on

to reach high academic and technical standards and even more had a sound foundation for career success in many fields. The school was often top of the divisional sports competitions and in athletics and soccer several pupils reached all-England standards."

Douglas Rimmer - Deputy Head

This local school was situated between the western perimeter of the Estate and the main road (Vicarage Road). The main entrance and playground facing the main road, its sports field and gardens at the rear. A primary, junior and secondary school all on the same site. As the result of considerable damage by incendiary bombs during the War; the infant class rooms were two wooden huts close to the main brick built, two story building; junior classes years 3,4, 5 and 6 in two prefab buildings on the edge of the sports field. During the severe winter of 1947 when it was so cold, the pupils in the prefabs had to be squeezed into makeshift classrooms within the main school. Junior classes 1 and 2 were in the main building on the ground floor. The toilet block stood alone, accessed to the main building by a covered area. All the temporary class rooms were heated by free standing coke stoves; replenished by the teachers during the day, with buckets of coke. Mr. Rudge the school caretaker maintained the stoves, filling the buckets from his fuel store in his boiler room in the main building, which was centrally heated.

The Estate children gained access to the school from its rear entrance which opened onto the cinder track that encircled the Estate - at the back of No. 56 where Pam and Carol Spence lived with their Mum and Dad, Charles and Gladys. The majority of the children started their education at Kenyngton Manor School; apart from one or two families who were Catholics and attended St. Ignatius, the school attached to the Catholic Church, a half a mile away. Very few went to private schools, and if they did, it was when they reached Junior or Senior age. At age 5 children could start school in September, January and Easter. Robert Kiss was 5 in February 1944, and started school at Easter, staying for school dinners; living at the end of the Estate it was too far to go home. Dinner money was taken to school on Monday - 2/1d - 5d a day. School Dinner not 'lunch' in those days.

Lynda Ross was 5 in June 1945 and started school in the September. She went home to dinner each day; her journey was short, across the road, down the alleyway next to Gordon Maile's house at No. 20, and into the school back gate. Running all the way, Lynda loved school, so always ran. If her mother Rose had gone to London for the day to visit relatives, then it was an even quicker route. On those days she would be having dinner at Dot Pead's, her mother's friend, with Andy and Susie Pead at No. 62; their back gate was opposite the school gate. It was a short journey through the school gardens, perhaps with time to have a quick run over and down the other side of the grassed old air raid shelters, used to store spare school desks and chairs. Very smelly, dark dank places, only entered when helping to carry chairs for Sports Day.

Robert Kiss remembers his first year in the juniors receiving two lashes of the cane on the hand at age 7 from the Headmaster Mr. Muncaster for throwing a potato or two at another boy at lunch time. At the end of that school year, in Form 2, Robert came 26th in the class of 45 - on his school report his teacher Miss Beckwith wrote -

"Robert likes to fool around too much, so his work suffers".

His father said if he came top in the next year he would buy him a new bicycle. The bicycle failed to arrive despite Robert achieving 1st place in Form 3. He entered Form 6, the 11+ year, still awaiting the bicycle and he failed the 11+. He completed his education at Kenyngton Manor Secondary school and was Head Boy in his final year. It was traditional for the Head Master to secure employment opportunities for the Head Boy and Robert was employed by Sunbury Urban District Council as a Junior Clerk in the Treasurers' Dept.

1948-1950 The Gap Years - Lynda Ross

"It is no good Lyn, you have to go" words spoken in anguish but none the less irrefutable and non-negotiable - I knew. There was no comforting hug, only the hand on my shoulder as I sobbed uncontrollably, my head buried in my arms on the kitchen worktop. I have no other memory of that day, subsequent day or what month it was but I know now the year was 1948 and I was 8 years old. My father was telling me I was going to live with my Grandmother, Nanny Jarvis who lived many miles away. I did know that my mother was ill but at that moment I do not remember any thought of the pain of leaving her or my baby sister; certainly not my Father who I had only known for three years. I was only consumed with the fear of having to go to a different school! Before this day I was aware that my mother spent every day on a bed in the sitting room in her red dressing gown - her dark medicine being poured drop by drop into a glass of water and watching it swirl in threads, dissolve and disappear. I remember the neighbour who kept goats on the land behind our house, calling with a supply of goats milk which my Mother had to drink each

day. It is the richest milk there is; my sister and I had a taste at the time, but never since. It was probably the same eventful day I remember my Father's distress trying to comfort my Mother as she implored him not to let the Doctor send her away to the sanatorium. I now know that she had been diagnosed with tuberculosis.

How long after that eventful day I do not know, but we did go - Mum to Harefield Hospital (later famous for heart surgery), my dear little baby sister Jill 18 months old, to London to be looked after by my Aunt Annie and family and me to Lymington in Hampshire. My mother's family rallied to help. Where were my father's family? Well Grandma and Grandad Ross lived just a few streets away, nearby my Father's brother, Uncle Bill, his wife Elsie and cousin Peter Ross. Aunty Elsie was my mother's best friend but when my Mother was diagnosed with TB Grandad Ross forbade any of the family to have any contact with us. Auntie Elsie had to obey her husband and my mother never spoke to her again. Grandad thought they would all catch TB and as a family we never spoke of them or to them again. At the time Peter Ross was in the same class as me at school but of course I went to Lymington.

Why do I not remember being taken on that journey? How did I get there? No one in the family had a car, it must have been by train and who took me? I will never know, there is no one left to ask. There are only my own memories of my life for two years in the care of a 73 year old widow who I hardly remembered before I was delivered to her. Of course I should have done so, for you see my Mother and I lived with her for the first five years of my life during the War. Christmas 1949 - my Mother recovered and returned home; we became a family again and I returned to school in Sunbury.

11+ Examination

Created by the 1944 Butler Education Act, an examination for children in their final year of primary education, taken between the ages of 10 and 11. There was an arithmetic test, an English test and an intelligence test to assess the ability to apply logic to simple problems. The result determined which type of secondary school a child would attend; a grammar school or a secondary modern. The majority of parents knew the importance of a grammar school education, the opportunity for their children to have a better education than they had received; many had left school at 14. They wanted them to pass the 11+ and the children too wanted to go to the Grammar School, especially if brothers and sisters were already there. Some found the money to pay for their children to receive private coaching in preparation for the examination. Michael Robbins, an only child, remembers the evenings when this strange man came to the house and his mother hauled him in from playing outside, much against his will. He then had to sit at the table answering questions from old test papers - he passed the 11+.

The day you learned whether you had passed the 11+ examination was a day you never forgot. The result envelopes were handed out - thick if you had passed, thin if not. Thick envelopes contained all the information about your new school, the grammar school to which you had been allocated with details of the uniform and equipment need, and travel passes. A thin envelope was just a letter to say you had failed. Brian Higgs can remember the day before the results came out. His class was segregated into two groups - one group on one side of the room, one on the other. He realised the next day one group was those who had passed the 11+, the other those who had failed - he was in the failed group. Some years later, Jacqui Clark from No. 32 missed taking the exam as she was suffering from Mumps. She had to take the exam on her own in the staff room the first morning she returned to school after two weeks absence.

You selected your school preference before taking the exam - the two best schools were considered to be Hampton Grammar for boys and Twickenham County for girls; the other two were Ashford County and Thames Valley, which were mixed grammar schools. Half the children on the Estate passed the 11+ and 13+ exams, the remaining half went to the Secondary Modern School. The majority of the boys went to Hampton Grammar, with just one or two going to Ashford County mixed school. Dorothy Linter No. 202, Pamela Martin No. 33 and Ruth Bulpit No. 140 went to Twickenham County Grammar school for girls, one or two went to Ashford. Lady Eleanor Hollis was a girls public school next door to Hampton Grammar and Eileen Cameron from No. 8 Beechwood Av. won a scholarship to go there when she passed the 11+. It is thought only two or three of the children went to university. Tony Burningham from No. 15 was one and at No. 147 Colin Oldacre who was a student at Nottingham University in the 1950s. In his work at university he was involved with a machine that could update the stock records of Boots the chemist in a four hour period and do the same task for a large section of the Army, in an equally fast time slot. It meant very little to us then but now we realise it was computing in its infancy. Don Wiley from No. 218 who went to Hampton Grammer, also went to university and subsequently became a dentist. Basil Miles No. 53 was educated *privately, worked for the National Provincial Bank, and was elected as a Councillor for Sunbury Urban District Council. He subsequently became Mayor of Spelthorne and his mother Gladys Miles was his Mayoress.*

13+ Examination

The 13+ examination was an opportunity for children at the Secondary Modern schools to receive a technical college education. Having an advantage over a grammar school education; on leaving school you were trained for a job. Sunbury children had the opportunity to go to Twickenham Technical College to study mechanical and electrical engineering and a branch at Hampton, the Commercial College, to study book-keeping, commerce and secretarial skills. Those wishing to study for the building trade went to Hammersmith School of Building. Eddie Walker and Brian Higgs travelled together to Hammersmith - quite a journey each way, two buses and an underground train journey. Lynda Ross passed the exam to go to Hampton and travelled there by bicycle.

The Drowning
Summer 1952 - Lynda Ross

The boy sat on the stage, head bowed, looking at his hands clasped in his lap; a man and a woman were sitting beside him - who were they? I knew that boy, he was in my class - it was Ronald Pateman - why was he sitting there? What had he done? Could that be his Mum and Dad with him? Mr. Dutton, the Headmaster, stood in his usual place behind the lectern. Mr. Dutton always took Assembly on the stage alone; this morning was obviously very different. There was complete silence in the Assembly Hall - something seemed wrong.

That Summer morning, as I always did, I had run down the alley way opposite our house, along the back of the houses and through the rear entrance to the school - I loved going to school and always ran. I made my way to the front of the building, looking across the playground to see if my friend Brenda had arrived. She came on the bus from Feltham. It was late coming that morning, so no time to talk before forming up in class lines in front of the main door, ready to march into morning assembly. Anyway talking in the lines was prohibited; if one did chatter it was one of the easiest ways to get sent to stand outside Mrs. Barratt's classroom and a possible cane across the hand. So we had all filed quietly into our class positions in the hall as usual but there was definitely something wrong, I could feel it in the silence.

Even Mr. Dutton's voice was different, perhaps because of the silence it was quieter than normal and seemed sad when he said his usual "Good Morning Children". In the Hall you could hear a pin drop. "Some of you, who were there, may know this already, but most of you do not and I have to tell you. Yesterday afternoon John Forey from Form 1A Upper was drowned whilst swimming in the River. This is a terrible tragedy for our school and as your Headmaster I want you to know what a true friend Ronald Pateman was to John. He put his own life at risk by diving several times under the water swimming in the weeds to find John and try to rescue him. Sadly he was unable to save his friend's life".

In the September Term 1951 I had returned to Kenyngton Manor School, not to the Primary School as before but to Form 1A Upper KM Secondary Modern. Not to the pre-fab class rooms on the playing field with their smelly coke

89

stoves but into the main school building. A rabbit warren of strange rooms those first days - a week or two before one felt at home running confidently between classes. Actually not running - forbidden - just changing class rooms for different subjects. Form 1A Upper had an uncomfortable class room - the Science Lab - sitting on high stools against work benches. This was because Mr. Morgan the Science Teacher was our form teacher. In the first week we were given our 'House' names - we were either in Sunbury, Thames, Valley or Middlesex. Blue, Red, Green and Yellow - but we did not have a choice which house we would like to be in. I was in 'Middlesex' - within a few weeks I soon realised I would rather be in 'Thames' as it was their red ribbon that seemed to always be tied around the monthly silver cup in the Trophy Cabinet and 'Middlesex' always last in the points table.

Mr. Jennings was the Metal Work teacher and also taught the boys gardening but one afternoon a week he took our class and Class 1B Lower, to Hounslow Swimming Baths to teach us to swim. I cannot remember how we got to the Swimming Baths; probably by coach, as the only other way of getting there would be a No. 237 bus. Can't see how we would have all fitted into a single decker bus! I could not swim when I started my lessons with Mr. Jennings but he was a good teacher and in a very short time I could manage a feeble breast stroke. The first thing he proved to us was that our bodies could float - he demonstrated this by putting his toes under the bar running along the side, stretched out his body, arms close to his side and then released his toes - and he did not sink! By the end of the second lesson I mastered floating on my back and with the confidence floating gave me, I was soon swimming after a fashion. Those of the class who could already swim were sent up to the deep end to enjoy themselves. The learners were at the shallow end but John Forey and I as 'floaters' soon got the confidence to be allowed to practice swimming strokes in the middle of the pool, on our own, not quite out of our depth, a toe touch to the bottom.

Sunbury open air swimming pool was on Rivermead Island on the River Thames, one of the few islands on the Thames that had public access by way of a narrow metal footbridge. Alongside was a ford where cars were able to cross - not that there were many cars in those days. In summer we would ride our bikes up to Sunbury Cross; when safe to cross over, ride over the railway bridge, up the Avenue and down Thames Street to the Island. It had been a hot summer the year I learnt to swim, there had been many trips to the pool with friends. You needed a sixpence to get in and one penny for a slice of bread and jam from Mr. Richard's tea kiosk next door.. We were always starving after swimming.

Some days we were successful in getting in for a swim, often it was full to bursting and the gates would be closed. 'Muscles' the life guard would stand guard at the gate trying to placate those who were shut out - "be patient and wait for the next session" . He would blow a whistle and eventually the pool would be emptied. It would be ages before all the reluctant children were hauled out of the pool, collected their towels and clothes and shooed outside to give others a turn. We often did not have the patience to wait and would ride around the back of the pool, making our way further down the Island to little sandy bays where we could paddle and swim in the River. This was strictly forbidden by our parents - there was always the danger of catching Polio from the river water. No inoculation then for this fearful disease. We were just desperate to cool off and swim so always lied when we got home. The River was deep and dangerous and us girls always just swam within the confines of the little bays. Handy tree branches growing out from the bank were there to clutch and we could still touch toes on the bottom. The boys, who always seemed such strong swimmers, would show off by swimming right across to the coal barges tied up on the other side, clamber aboard and dive off. "Dare you sissies to come over too!" they would shout.

That fateful afternoon John Carey, not a strong swimmer, just like me, had taken a dare and with his friends he tried to swim across to the coal barges. Something happened, and it is said he disappeared under the water half-way across. Ronald Pateman standing on the coal barge saw his best friend disappear under the water and not re-surface. He dived off the barge, swam to the middle of the river and dived repeatedly, desperately trying to find him.

On the last day of term in July 1952 we were all at morning assembly and again Ronald Pateman and his parents were sitting on the stage. Mr. Dutton the Headmaster introduced a very official looking gentleman. "Children, this is Mr. Chamberlain, from the Royal Humane Society, who on behalf of the President, the H.R.H. the Duke of Gloucester, is here to present to Ronald Pateman, the Society's Honorary Testimonial. I would like to read to you all that is enscribed on the testimonial. 'It was resolved unanimously that the Honorary Testimonial of this Society, inscribed on parchment be hereby given to Ronald Pateman for having at personal risk, gone to the rescue of his best friend John Forey, who was unfortunately drowned in the River Thames at Sunbury and whose life he gallantly attempted to save".

Hampton School of Commerce - Lynda Ross

As "the crow flies" I lived too near the school to have a free bus pass. Money was short at home and bus fares difficult to find, also the money for the purchase of a bicycle. A second-hand bike appeared just in time before the start of term in September - it had been given to me by a work colleague of Dad's. His daughter was very ill and unable to use the machine any more. I treasured that bike - it was a Raleigh Sports model with thin tyres and drop handle bars, unlike my friends' bicycles. I used to call for Sheila Simmons at No. 232 and Sylvia Wynn from nearby Cavendish Road, joined us for the ride to school. Sylvia was expelled at the end of the last Spring term for smoking behind the bicycle sheds. One morning she had the bad luck of being discovered by a stranger wandering about the school grounds. She told him to mind his own business but it turned out to be a schools' inspector. After we completed three years study at the college, we emerged as fully qualified, unexperienced shorthand typists. Some of us had the opportunity to take 'O' level examinations in our final year and I managed to gain a pass in six subjects. As a result I was offered a place in the 6th form at Twickenham County Grammar school. I was thrilled as I really wanted to continue my studies and become a school teacher but news of the opportunity was not welcomed at home and I was told I would be leaving school and starting work.

Starting Work

Lynda Ross

In the late 1950s 'Rackmanism' was rife. Peter Rackman

93

built a property empire in London and was notorious in the Nottinghill Area of London for driving out mostly white, sitting tenants, who had statutory protection against high rent increases; and then filled the properties with recent immigrants from the West Indies. New tenants did not have the same protection under the law as had previous ones and so could be charged any amount of rent Rachman wished. The immigrants had no choice but to accept the high rents, as it was difficult to obtain housing in London at the time. My parents, together with many other families living on our estate, became very concerned about the future, with the prospect of rents rising out of control. The subsequent Rent Act 1965 gave security to tenants, but had the unintended consequence that private rented housing became scarce.

Early in 1956, the year I left school, my Father had taken the bold step of giving in his notice to W.H.Smith and accepting employment with Mr. Meyer, a friend who had a bookshop. Mum and Dad decided to buy their house as sitting tenants for £1,500 and remove the threat of being unable to manage a higher rent. The superannuation Dad received on leaving W.H.Smith's, was used for a deposit, and they entered into a mortgage agreement with the Liverpool & Victoria Insurance Company. Having just left college and started work as a Secretary on a salary of £5 per week, I had been asked to contribute £2 of this a week as board and lodging and help towards the mortgage repayments. I did not want to work locally and looked in the newspaper for jobs in London. I obtained an interview to be a shorthand typist with the Royal London Insurance Co. in the City of London. My interview was conducted in a huge room with rows and rows of girls working on typewriters. My shorthand was not very good and I failed *the interview but was offered a position as a clerk. Having had a day off from school, I returned the next day with my tail between my legs and was summoned to the Headmaster's office to tell him the result of my interview. I have a very clear memory of that morning. He looked me in the eye and said*

"You are not suited to that sort of position. Your GCE predictions are good and I have every confidence in you becoming more than just a shorthand typist in the future. As Headmaster I am approached by employers who wish to employ my students. I have been asked to find a suitable candidate for a secretarial position in the small practice of a Chartered Accountant in the City of London. If you agree I will arrange for you to have an interview."

I was more successful this time and was offered the position. The following day was Sports Day and I remember running across the field to find the Headmaster. I blurted out to him the success of the previous day and the fact that I was going to be paid £5 per week - he looked at me and said

"The money is not important, are you going to be happy working there?"

I travelled up to London every day on the train to Waterloo. From there I caught the Drain, the fast one stop underground train service to the City of London. On the first part of my journey, on the train to Waterloo, I joined several other Ashridge Way girls on their way to work in London. With other friends we nearly filled a carriage - Eileen Cameron, now an Articled Clerk in a City Accountants firm, and Geraldine Pool from No. 14

Woodbury Close serving an apprenticeship with Constance Spry, the well-known London florist (the florist for the 2011 Royal Wedding) Hazel Rudge from Burgoyne Rd. also joined us every morning. She was engaged to a handsome Royal Navy officer. One morning she was missing from the train, we later learnt she and fiance had gone to Grena Green to get married. A friend of Geraldine's, Bernice, joined us in the carriage at Twickenham station. A very striking, attractive girl, her boyfriend was a member of Lonny Donegan's skiffle band; performing then at Eel Pie island on the Thames at Twickenham. She taught us the words to "My Old Man's a Dustman" before it was top of the charts. Fred Jackson was the eldest of the Jackson family living at No. 1 Woodbury Close. He worked in a bank in London and was the only male who joined us every morning in our railway carriage. He was 21, older than us girls and rather superior. He was missing one morning; we learned he had been called up as an Army reservist for the Suez crisis, and was parachuted into the desert as part of the attempt by the Western allies to gain control of the canal. We were surprised to see him back with us within the month - he had broken his ankle when he was parachuted in and had been sent home. He was a member of the 5th Sunbury Rover Crew and they remember him arriving unexpectedly back into their fold on their meeting night - he told them he was paid sixty-six pounds, six shillings and six pence for that tour of duty.

5th Sunbury Scout Troop

"The scout hut was always part of my life and I worked my way through the cubs, scouts, senior scouts, Rovers and as an assistant Scout Leader" *Derek Chapman*

96

From its beginnings in 1943 and to date, the 5th Sunbury Scout Troop has been an integral part of the lives of the families who lived in River Gardens; in the early years most of the boys who belonged to this Scout Troop lived on the estate. The Wolf cub pack and Scout Troop first met in Kenyngton Manor school hall and on Wednesday evenings from 6-8 the Rev. George Elcock vicar at St. Saviours Church, organised games for the scouts in the loft space of a motor car repair garage in Staines Road West, close to Sunbury Cross Parade. Hot dusty fun ending with a cup of tea and a bun. George was a great scout loved by all. In the late 1940s the Metropolitan Water Board leased the Scouts a piece of land in the Jungle. Arthur Britton ('Gaffer') from No. 162 was Group Scout Master, Jack Starr ('Skip') Scout Master. The two Assistant Scout Masters were 'Paddy' Miles and Reg Oldacre. Don Baird was Chairman of the Executive Committee for many years. Together they organised a working party of Scout's fathers to clear the site and help build a Scout hut. It was open for meetings in 1950. Each Scout patrol had their own small activity/camp site bordering the camp fire circle - Stags, Wolves, Kestrel and Foxes. Regular camp fires were held during weekend camps, always led by 'Skip' and Vernon - the verger at St.Saviours. Vernon always produced a Billy Bunter tale to enthrall the boys with voices to add character to his 'stunt'. Cubs occasionally went summer camp to sites in the nearby Surrey countryside. The Scout Troop always had a summer camp at sites in Sussex or Hampshire. More often than not an Easter/Whitsun camp was held nearby at Walton Firs, a National Scout Association camp site.

As the boys grew older so the Troop grew; at 15 years of age they became Senior Scouts and then onto Rover Scouts at 18. In 1956 a group of Senior Scouts and Rovers made their first trip abroad. A ten day holiday staying in youth hostels in West Germany and Belgium. Holland was on the itinery but due to a polio outbreak this part of the trip was cancelled and more time was spent in Germany. A lasting memory was seeing the extensive war damage on buildings as their train pulled into into Aachen railway station.

Occasionally fund raising dances were organised; held in the school hall with music provided by 'The Grasshoppers' - 'Gaffa' on the drums, 'Skip' played the fiddle with Arkela's boyfriend on the piano. These events were always well supported by the parents and children. It was a few years later, in the late 1950s, Old Time and Modern dancing lessons were held on Monday evenings in the Scout Hut; the tutor was Ron Brookes from No. 133. Parents and teenagers became proficient in the foxtrot, waltz and quickstep and the bigger variety of Old Time dances. Firmer friendships developed among the teenage dancing partners; strengthened by absence when the boys were called up for National Service. As boys reached eighteen, most of those who lived on the Estate completed the two years National Service; only a few were deferred or failed the medical examination. John Maudesley No. 176 served and was killed in Korea. Ernie Hodges was the only child of Ernie and Louisa Hodges at No. 132 and was killed on his motorcycle returning to barracks at Aldershot early one Monday morning. The whole estate mourned the death of these young men. Brian Thompson from No. 143 was one of last to be called up for National Service in the Army and served in Aden.

Marriage

It has already been recorded that grandparents and extended families settled in River Gardens. By the 1960s the children had become adults and several families became joined by marriage.

Joe Paynter at No. 228 married Lily Parker the girl next door at No. 226.

Neil Harrison from No. 66 married Rosemary Burningham from No. 15. They went to live in South Africa but sadly Rosemary was killed in a car accident shortly afterwards.

An extra-large clan - they even had Scottish names - was created on the Estate when Jill Ross married Keith Baird in April 1967. Joining these families together by marriage .

No. 49 Ralph

No. 51 Chapman

No. 57 Ross

No. 101 Baird

No. 134 Robbins

No. 185 Kiss

In August 1961 Jill's sister, Lynda Ross had married Robert Kiss. Robert and Lynda bought No. 1 The Vale when Robert's grandmother Katie Kiss gave up the tenancy. They had their first daughter Katie in 1966 and moved away in 1968.

Susan Feather from No. 1 married Don Oestal at No. 118.

Her brother Russell married Susan Farmer from No. 139.

In 1971 John Gridley at No. 117 married Mavis Bright who lived next door at No. 119. His daughter Helen now lives in No. 119 after her grandmother Florence Bright died in 2003. John's grandson goes to 5th Sunbury Scouts.

In 1972 the property company Freehold Building & Land Dev.Co.Ltd. sold the River Gardens property investment, to Equity & Estate Investment Co. Ltd. The rent being paid at the time was around £5.50p per week, some had 25p reduction for lack of garage space. The new owners were proposing to increase the rent to £7.75 per week. It is known that a protest meeting of tenants was held at No. 123 John Richards house. When John Richards died, his son found among other family papers, a schedule showing the names and house numbers, of those who attended the meeting. It lists 52 families still renting their property but it is not known if this is a complete record as all may not have attended the meeting.

PART SIX

Conclusion

"I remember the day they started digging up our field and turning it into a Council House Estate. Such a sad day"
Eileen Inseal

In 1950 on the 15 acre plot of fields in Beechwood Avenue, a Council House building project was begun. The scheme included terrace houses, semi-detached pairs, flats and single-story dwellings for old people. The architects were Basil Spence & Partners and were of a very utilitarian design. As Sir Basil Spence, the architect did move on to greater things. These new properties had aluminum roofs that shone in the sun and more often than not glistened in the rain. A few years later, during an exceptional storm, one or two of the roofs peeled off like a tin of sardines. Comparing photographs one could not say that these new homes blended well with their neighbours; the 'Tudor' and 'Suntrap' styles of the 'Vincent' houses in River Gardens. Albert Charles Cowtan was the architect for River Gardens; a man who had interrupted his architectural training with active service in France in WW1 and continued at Regent St. Polytechnic after the War, eventually obtaining his own small architectural practice in Leatherhead, Surrey.

It is true, it was sad the children lost a large part of the open space they had previously enjoyed as their adventure playground but they still had the Orchard behind their own houses to call their own and happily shared it with the new influx of children and made lots of new friends.

"Such a happy place to grow up! My best pal Anne Myers

and family lived at 103 Ashridge Way. Such fun, football and cricket matches on the 'Ring' and adventures in the Jungle. Alexis Gilmour was born at No. 36 Beechwood Av. the first Council terrace.

The new homes were desperately needed of course and the River Gardens residents welcomed the new arrivals. Nimbyism was not a word heard at this time. It was a slow process in those early post war years for families to rebuild their lives after the devastation of War and houses were needed for the 'baby boomers' . Families in River Gardens had relatives who were able to rent these new houses with gardens instead of living in a flat with small children. Two sisters Margaret Tresaden and Evelyn Gregory were thrillled to be given a new house near to their brother and other sister Joan Robbins. Their Mother Katie Kiss living in The Vale, was able to see more of her grandchildren. Lynda Ross now had Grandad and Grandma Ross living happily in one of the single-story dwellings for the elderly; they had moved from the larger house they previously rented in Heathcroft Avenue.

The Coronation street party had been held just in time, a few years later the Council gobbled up more land and Keywood Drive another housing development was built around the 'Ring' and the Orchard disappeared under bricks and mortar. Fortunately they left the grassed area in the centre to remain as a small play area for the new residents. River Gardens was no longer "in a background of rural splendour", as quoted in the sales brochure..

The spirit of the River Gardens community was probably at it zenith in the weeks and months following victory in 1945. It remained strong for some years but naturally it changed to accommodate the welcome peace. When children who had grown up through the War years married and moved away from the area in the later 1950s and 1960s, much of the vitality went with them. The older generation who stayed continued their own social lives into retirement but their numbers dwindled with time and they became a peripheral group as a new move-in community steadily replaced them. Minnie Chapman, a widow after 1970 died in 1987 aged 83. Florrie and Don Baird both lived into their early 90s and were just about the last of the original Ashridge Way residents when they moved out into more appropriate accommodation in 1991. In 1983 Albert and Rose Ross moved to a retirement bungalow in Everton Nr. Lymington on the South Coast and Bill and Chris Kiss also moved to Hampshire and enjoyed many happy years living near their grandchildren. Bill Norman still lives at No. 88 where his parents brought him to live aged 6 in 1937. John Butcher returned to No. 116 where he was born and now cares for his mother Margaret Butcher aged 97 who came to live there with her husband Stanley in 1938. Dorothy Linter still lives at No. 202, travelling to London one day a week to work as a volunteer at Bart's Hospital in London. This is where she qualified as a nurse and worked until retirement.

Today the 1930s style of houses still appeal to young married couples. Sadly the River Gardens Estate as a whole has not maintained its "neatness and charm" as advertised in its sales brochure. Another quote from the brochure "the provision of garage access by right of way at rear, without which no house in future years will be saleable" now has little relevance. Increased car ownership resulted in cars being parked on both sides of the road, to such an extent that it was reaching a situation where a one way system *through the estate would be necessary. With only one entrance and exit to a housing development that had more than doubled in size; health and safety issues had to be addressed to ensure quick access for ambulances and fire engines. The Council's solution was to widen the road by the removal of the grass verges. Many householders have now removed the low brick walls, concreted over their front gardens, had kerbs lowered and now have space to park several cars.*

This chronicle began when Sunbury-on-Thames was a small village but it ends when it could no longer be described as such. During the 1960s it had grown significantly with many housing developments, a subsequent increase in population and expansion of local industries. On the 1st April 1965 Sunbury became part of Surrey, when the ancient county of Middlesex was abolished and absorbed into the new county of Greater London. A more dramatic change took place when the flyover for the M3 motorway was built, the landmark of Sunbury Cross and its Clock Tower was replaced by a roundabout. The Clock Tower now sat insignificantly within a forest of sky scraper shops and offices under the flyover. Its stay was brief, within a few years concerned residents had it moved to a more venerable position. There is no longer an open air swimming pool on Rivermead Island. This amenity was closed in 1980 and no trace of it now remains.

The Preface to this book explains the reason why these memories, in my view, should be recorded. In recent decades, families, households and living arrangements have gone through major changes. In particular the patterns of family formation, dissolution and re-

104

constitution have become more heterogeneous and family boundaries more ambiguous. This account records the lives of strong family units, how they survived a war, came through the other side and faced the future with optimism and hope. Their children had the advantage of living in "rural splendour" a perfect environment. In my search for material to add to my own and my husband's recollections, I have been overwhelmed with the support, encouragement and enthusiasm I have received for my project from long standing childhood friends, previous neighbours and grandchildren who all remember life in that community with affection. We were a privileged group, our parents had confidence and faith in the future to make a new start in an unfamiliar environment for them but which was perfect for us.

Lynda Kiss

Notes

1.   Sunbury-on-Thames *"one of those pleasant villages lying on the Thames, near Hampton Court"* Gilbert White 1767. Historically in Middlesex forming the Sunbury-on-Thames Urban District Council from 1894. In 1965, when most of Middlesex was absorbed into Greater London, Sunbury was transferred to Surrey.

2.   Poupart Jam Co. By the middle of the nineteenth century William Poupart and his family were selling their produce in the London markets from their farms at Twickenham and Walton-on-Thames. Early market gardeners had produced and sold their own crops but as the London markets grew they had to travel to the City and market their produce. William Poupart 1847-1930 became an expert on fruit and was a judge for the Royal Horticultural Society. The Poupart company has evolved and developed. It moved from a single proprietor business, growing and marketing its own produce, to being part of a major food group, representing growers from the UK and around the World with an annual turnover in excess of £340 million.

3.   Kempton Park Pumping Station. In its listed engine house are two magnificant Worthington-Simpson, large triple-expansion steam engines 1926-1927. Each one is of similar size to that used in RMS Titanic. Each pumped 19 million gallons of water a day to supply North London with drinking water, taken from the River Thames. They are thought to be the biggest ever built in the UK and the last working survivors when they were retired from service in

1980. One of the engines is called The Sir William Prescott and has been restored to running order. It is the largest fully operational triple-expansion steam engine in the world. It may be seen in steam on various weekends during the year at the museum operated by Kempton Great Engine Trust. www.kemptonsteam.org.

4.   River Ash Is a distributory of the River Colne running through the towns of Staines and Ashford - which gained its name from the river. Maps featuring the Ash date to medieval times. The course of the river has been much influenced by human action. It joins the River Thames in the Creek upstream of Sunbury Lock Island.

PART TWO

The Breadwinners

1.   British Thermostat In 1928 Teddington Refrigeration Controls/Teddington Appliance Controls were set up in Teddington with a payroll of four, producing controls and automatic thermostats. The Company was known as British Termostat Co. Ltd. and by 1931 had expanded greatly and moved to new premises at Sunbury-on-Thames. In 1934 the Company collaborated with Rolls-Royce to produce an experimental thermostat for their cars and a system that became the forerunner of nearly every system fitted to the Merlin engines during the war and other equipment for the Spitfire and Hurricane. During the War they had a payroll of 2,300.

2.   Rolls Royce In 1906 Charles Stewart Rolls and Henry Royce founded the renowned car manufacturing company and later aero-engine manufacturing company. Around half of the aircraft engines used by the Allies in WW1 were made by Rolls-Royce. By the late 1920s aero engines made up most of Rolls-Royce's business. Henry Royce's

3.   last design was the Merlin, a powerful supercharged V12 engine and fitted into many

4.   WW2 aircraft, including the Spitfire and the Hawker Hurricane. It crossed over into

5.   military land-vehicle use as the Meteor powering the Centurian tank.

6.   Anglo Iranian Oil Co. The first company to extract petroleum from Iran was Anglo-Persian Oil Co. - renamed in 1935 to the Anglo Iranian Oil Co. In 1954 it became the Brtish Petroleum Co. (BP).

7.   R.C.A. Radio Corporation of America the American electronics company 1919-1986.

In 1930 the company began selling the first electronic turntable and in 1949 RCA released the first 45rpm record to the public, competing with Columbia's 33⅓rpm LP.

8.   Cantrell & Cochrane 1852 Dr. Thomas Cantrell opened a shop in Belfast selling soft drinks, going into partnership with Alderman Henry Cochrane and thereafter trading as Cantrell & Cochrane Ltd. Today it is C&Cgroup plc.

9.   Sundeala now operates from Dursley in Gloucestershire "A Company committed to recycling" producing environmentally sustainable board manufacured from 100% waste paper.

10.   Ford Motor Co. In 1917 the company opened its assembly plants in England and by 1919 was producing 40% of all British cars. Bill Kiss served his apprenticeship in their plant at Dagenham which opened in 1931.

11.   H.J.Mulliner & Co. a well-known British coachbuilder. It can trace its history back to 1760 building coaches for the Royal Mail in Northampton. By the 1930s virtually its entire output was being fitted to Rolls-Royce and Bentley cars. Rolls-Royce acquired Mulliner in 1959.

12.   Vickers Armstrong the aviation department was formed in 1911. Supermarine Aviation Works (Vickers) Ltd. was responsible for producing the revolutionary Spitfire fighter. Bill Kiss, having worked on the Spitfire during the War, returned to working in the aircraft industry in 1960. He was employed by Hawker Siddley at Kingston in their experimental department; firstly on the development of the Harrier Jump Jet and then on the production of the Hawk, the advanced training jet for the Royal Air Force.

 He was a skilled worker and retired from the Company aged 68.

13.   Kingston Power Station was a coal-fired generating station on the Thames at Kingston-upon-Thames. The river was used both for coal supply and ash removal as well as a source of cooling water. It ceased operating 1980 and the station was eventually demolished, despite calls for preservation as power museum. The two 250ft chimneys were demolished in 1994.

14.   Battersea Power Station is now a decommissioned coal-fired power station on the south bank of the River Thames at Battersea. It ceased generating electricity in

1983 but it is one of the best known land marks in London and is a Grade II listed building. It is the largest brick building in Europe. The building of the A Station was begun in 1929, once the steel frame was completed the construction of the brick cladding began in 1931. Its control room was given many Art Deco fittings. Italian marble was used for the turbine hall and wrought iron staircases were used throughout. Owing to the lack of money following WW2, the interior of the B Station was not given the same treatment and fittings were made of stainless steel.

15.   Nettlefold Studios An early film pioneer, Cecil Hepworth started the Hepworth Studios in 1899 in a house in Walton-on-Thames. In 1926 the studios were bought by Archibald Nettlefold and renamed the Nettlefold Studios. They made comedy silents until it was upgraded to sound in the early 1930s. During the Second World War the buildings were used as storage by the government and the Vickers-Armstrong aircraft company built two new hangers due to a direct hit by an enemy bomb at their nearby factory in Kingston-on-Thames. In 1955 Sapphire Films eventually bought the studios, renaming them Walton Studios. Unable to compete with other studios they closed in 1961 and most of the equipment was sold to Shepperton Studios and many of the 200 employees moved there.

Acknowledgements

My first thanks go to Word Play and its founders Ian Govan and Michael Barton. Being a member of Word Play Writers Forum I have been encouraged to write and more than that helped to get published through its self-publishing company; dedicated to helping writers see their work come to the market and get read.

Also the support and encouragement of Ken Smallbone, Editor of Hampshire Genealogical Society and source for the Preface. National Archives Podcast 'Writing a history of one's own times' Prof.Peter Hennessy.

I am most grateful to Brenda Horwill who lives in Sunbury and without whose help I would not have made contact with so many of the previous residents and families of River Gardens; especially for making the poster she displayed in Sunbury Library. Her continued help over the past few months; answering questions, scanning material and being supportive in every way. Six years ago, Brenda's 'Kenyngton Manor' group on Friends Reunited created a dialogue with old school friends and the germ of an idea for this book. Two sessions of brain storming with Ben Richards in his New York apartment resulted in mapping nearly all the houses of our childhood friends in River Gardens - thanks Ben for your hospitality and contributions to the memories. On a visit to Brisbane in 2006, we renewed our friendship with Eileen and Marion Inseal, fifty years after the family emigrated to Australia - thank you both and brother Fred; your reminiscences on that occasion and in correspondence since, are all recorded in these pages.

Becky Middleton of the Herald & News/Staines Informer kindly published my letter about the book. This resulted in my being contacted by Bill Norman who provided the amazing 'gift' of an original sales brochure for 'Vincent Houses'. Thank you Bill for allowing me to re-produce this jewel, which brought to life my description of these special homes. The professional help provided by photographer, Steve Fuller, has resulted in the brochure pages being reproduced perfectly in spite of their fragile condition. The RIBA and Justine Sambrook, Curator of the Robert Elwall Photographs Collection were particularly supportive to me in my research into the Architect of the River Gardens Estate and the later Council development. Also Crittall Windows who were most helpful in contacting Jennifer Brown of Braintree District Museum.

Sunbury & Shepperton History Society for providing the Sunbury Swimming Pool photograph and special thanks to their officers Nick Pollard and Peter Bailey for their prompt replies to enquiries on WW2 research. Monica Chard Editor of 'Sunbury Matters' for including my article, resulting in contact by Kenneth Battle (appropriately named!) who provided very useful facts about the V2 bomb. What would I have done without Wikipedia (I have made a donation); enabling me to find Kempton Great Engine Trust www.kemptonsteam.org, and all the information for my Notes. Surrey Comet Newspaper - 6.2.1980 for the obituary of Percy Dutton.

Warmest thanks to Ted Ralph (90) and his son Chris, they drove two hours across country to meet up with me during the busy summer holidays; to exchange valuable facts and memories of 50 years ago. Chris has been very supportive and encouraging in the editing and content of my book,

112

together with his brother Jon, and shared many family photographs. It was a privilege to meet Margaret Butcher (aged 97). Her son John brought her to meet me when I was in Sunbury this summer and I was pleased to use his map and memories. It was good to travel to Wales to meet Brian Higgs again after 50 years. Being one of the older children, Brian was able to fill in some of the gaps in the War years.

5th Sunbury Scouting days were recalled with Derek Chapman, Graham Hopkins, Basil Miles, Mike Robbins and John Gridley. Ted Edwards sadly died in October, shortly after sharing memories by email. Facebook was invaluable in making contact with some of those already acknowledged. The creation of an Ashridge Way group also put me in touch with the following children and grandchildren. Their enthusiasm and encouragement inspired me to record for us all, the "best years of our life" "very happy times for us all" - without their memories this book would be very dull reading!

Sue Knight (nee Robinson), Jose Cheshner (nee Robinson), Jacquie Gardner (nee Clark), Anthony Maskall, Brian Foster, Alan Hourd, Robert Fendle, Terry Pattison, Dorothy Linter, Donald Wiley, Peter Baker, Emily Parker (nee Kemp), Brian & Jackie Appleby, Joya Childs (nee Benaardout), Rae Johnson, Peter & Janet Freeman, Mike Rimmer, Jenny Clark, Alexis Gilmour, Janet Scammell (nee Green), Brian Marshall, Greg Spence, his sisters Carol and Pamela and his nephew Steve Fuller.

Last but not least, my love and thanks to my husband Robert Kiss, who is my biggest fan. Without his support and encouragement this book would not have been written but more importantly are his contributions about a childhood in Ashridge Way. After all there were gaps in the time I lived there and he and others have filled the pages, but it seems to me there were more children living at his end of the estate and more going on!

About the Author

Lynda was born in Sunbury-on-Thames in 1940. With a commercial college education, her working life was in secretarial employment in the City of London. In 1961 she married Robert Kiss. Whilst bringing up their children, two daughters and a son; Lynda gained an Open University Degree in Social Science. In the later years of employment Lynda was the Librarian at IBM's Science Laboratory in Winchester and was part of the editorial team of IBM Laboratories, for their in house magazine 'Developments'.

Particularly fortunate as a young child to have a constant supply of books, reading and writing have always been her main relaxation. With a preference for writing non-fiction, Lynda has written several articles for magazines on craft and cookery and in recent years with her interest in Family History, she has contributed to several Family History Society journals.

This is Lynda's first book; a project not just documenting but writing with pride what these families were able to accomplish and their contribution to what we are and have today.

Other books from WordPlay

Precinct Murder
by Various Authors

New York: the city where killers never sleep. For those that like their murder stories potted, this is the perfect coffee table crime anthology.

WordPlay ShowCase
by Various Authors

A collection of works by a series of writers, for some of whom this represents their first time in print. The anthology covers a whole range of writing: factual, fiction, social commentary, and poetry.

Shorts for Autumn
by Various Writers

The ideal accompaniment to an autumn evening spent by the fire, or that morning coffee break when you need to unwind and relax, Shorts for Autumn is a collection of fiction to suit all tastes, whether they be murder, romance, ghostly tales or just a little light humour.

Losing Hope
by Nikki Dee

In 1995 a small girl vanished from her home. No trace of her was found though her family never stopped looking. In 2010 a damaged and vulnerable young woman is rescued from a burning building. Can this possibly be that long lost child and, if so, where has she been and why?

The Cardinals of Schengen

by Michael Barton

Jack Hudson, the UK Government's Foreign Secretary, is assassinated in his own home. In attempting to discover his brother's murderer, Peter Hudson finds himself in a race against time to save Europe from a secret society determined to see Europe become the Fourth Reich.

My Gentle War (Memoirs of an Essex Girl)

by Joy Lennick

This is the true story of a young girl whose family is wrenched apart by the heartache and tragedy of World War II. Community spirit and togetherness see her through the worst of times, and welcomes in the best of times.

Divine Damages

by Georgia Varjas

This is a collection of ten elegant stories about the ends and means women will go to get even. Justice and sweet revenge has never been served quite so divinely as it is in this mischievous, ironic, and downright satisfying read. Bound to leave you fulfilled and gratified.

Keep Write On

by Ian Govan

Published posthumously, *Keep Write On* is a collection of Ian's musings on life and, in particular, writing. There is wit, tinged with, perhaps, a little life cynicism here and there, that will make you giggle inside. All royalties from sales will be used by WordPlay toward 'encouraging writers to write, and then getting them read'.

Fallyn and the Dragons

by K J Rollinson

A magical adventure that sees Allan, Eileen and Martin called away from the 'real world' to a medieval 'dream world'. There Allan is known as Lord Fallyn, and he and his friends go to the rescue of King Rudri's dragons and battle against Prince Bato who seeks to depose his brother. This is the first of the Fallyn Trilogy, with the second instalment, *Fallyn in the Forbidden Land*, also available on Amazon and Kindle.

Printed in Great Britain
by Amazon

79452845R00078